AI Self-Driving Cars Evolvement

Practical Advances in
Artificial Intelligence and Machine Learning

Dr. Lance B. Eliot, MBA, PhD

Disclaimer: This book is presented solely for educational and entertainment purposes. The author and publisher are not offering it as legal, accounting, or other professional services advice. The author and publisher make no representations or warranties of any kind and assume no liabilities of any kind with respect to the accuracy or completeness of the contents and specifically disclaim any implied warranties of merchantability or fitness of use for a particular purpose. Neither the author nor the publisher shall be held liable or responsible to any person or entity with respect to any loss or incidental or consequential damages caused, or alleged to have been caused, directly or indirectly, by the information or programs contained herein. Every company is different and the advice and strategies contained herein may not be suitable for your situation.

 First Edition.

ISBN: 1-7329760-8-2
ISBN-13: 978-1-7329760-8-5

DEDICATION

To my incredible son, Michael, and my incredible daughter, Lauren.

Forest fortuna adiuvat (from the Latin; good fortune favors the brave).

CONTENTS

ACKNOWLEDGMENTS

I have been the beneficiary of advice and counsel by many friends, colleagues, family, investors, and many others. I want to thank everyone that has aided me throughout my career. I write from the heart and the head, having experienced first-hand what it means to have others around you that support you during the good times and the tough times.

To Warren Bennis, one of my doctoral advisors and ultimately a colleague, I offer my deepest thanks and appreciation, especially for his calm and insightful wisdom and support.

To Mark Stevens and his generous efforts toward funding and supporting the USC Stevens Center for Innovation.

To Lloyd Greif and the USC Lloyd Greif Center for Entrepreneurial Studies for their ongoing encouragement of founders and entrepreneurs.

To Peter Drucker, William Wang, Aaron Levie, Peter Kim, Jon Kraft, Cindy Crawford, Jenny Ming, Steve Milligan, Chis Underwood, Frank Gehry, Buzz Aldrin, Steve Forbes, Bill Thompson, Dave Dillon, Alan Fuerstman, Larry Ellison, Jim Sinegal, John Sperling, Mark Stevenson, Anand Nallathambi, Thomas Barrack, Jr., and many other innovators and leaders that I have met and gained mightily from doing so.

Thanks to Ed Trainor, Kevin Anderson, James Hickey, Wendell Jones, Ken Harris, DuWayne Peterson, Mike Brown, Jim Thornton, Abhi Beniwal, Al Biland, John Nomura, Eliot Weinman, John Desmond, and many others for their unwavering support during my career.

And most of all thanks as always to Michael and Lauren, for their ongoing support and for having seen me writing and heard much of this material during the many months involved in writing it. To their patience and willingness to listen.

INTRODUCTION

This is a book that provides the newest innovations and the latest Artificial Intelligence (AI) advances about the emerging nature of AI-based autonomous self-driving driverless cars. Via recent advances in Artificial Intelligence (AI) and Machine Learning (ML), we are nearing the day when vehicles can control themselves and will not require and nor rely upon human intervention to perform their driving tasks (or, that <u>allow</u> for human intervention, but only *require* human intervention in very limited ways).

Similar to my other related books, which I describe in a moment and list the chapters in the Appendix A of this book, I am particularly focused on those advances that pertain to self-driving cars. The phrase "autonomous vehicles" is often used to refer to any kind of vehicle, whether it is ground-based or in the air or sea, and whether it is a cargo hauling trailer truck or a conventional passenger car. Though the aspects described in this book are certainly applicable to all kinds of autonomous vehicles, I am focused more so here on cars.

Indeed, I am especially known for my role in aiding the advancement of self-driving cars, serving currently as the Executive Director of the Cybernetic AI Self-Driving Cars Institute.. In addition to writing software, designing and developing systems and software for self-driving cars, I also speak and write quite a bit about the topic. This book is a collection of some of my more advanced essays. For those of you that might have seen my essays posted elsewhere, I have updated them and integrated them into this book as one handy cohesive package.

You might be interested in companion books that I have written that provide additional key innovations and fundamentals about self-driving cars. Those books are entitled **"Introduction to Driverless Self-Driving Cars,"** "**Advances in AI and Autonomous Vehicles: Cybernetic Self-Driving Cars,**" "**Self-Driving Cars: "The Mother of All AI Projects," "Innovation and Thought Leadership on Self-Driving Driverless Cars," "New Advances in AI Autonomous Driverless Self-Driving Cars," "Autonomous Vehicle Driverless Self-Driving Cars and Artificial Intelligence," "Transformative Artificial Intelligence**

Driverless Self-Driving Cars," "Disruptive Artificial Intelligence and Driverless Self-Driving Cars, and **"State-of-the-Art AI Driverless Self-Driving Cars,"** and **"Top Trends in AI Self-Driving Cars,"** and **"AI Innovations and Self-Driving Cars," "Crucial Advances for AI Driverless Cars," "Sociotechnical Insights and AI Driverless Cars," "Pioneering Advances for AI Driverless Cars"** and **"Leading Edge Trends for AI Driverless Cars," "The Cutting Edge of AI Autonomous Cars"** and **"The Next Wave of AI Self-Driving Cars"** and **"Revolutionary Innovations of AI Self-Driving Cars,"** and **"AI Self-Driving Cars Breakthroughs," "Trailblazing Trends for AI Self-Driving Cars," "Ingenious Strides for AI Driverless Cars," "AI Self-Driving Cars Inventiveness," "Visionary Secrets of AI Driverless Cars," "Spearheading AI Self-Driving Cars," "Spurring AI Self-Driving Cars," "Avant-Garde AI Driverless Cars,"** and **"AI Self-Driving Cars Evolvement"** (they are all available via Amazon). Appendix A has a listing of the chapters covered in those books.

For the introduction herein to this book, I am going to borrow my introduction from those companion books, since it does a good job of laying out the landscape of self-driving cars and my overall viewpoints on the topic. The remainder of the book is all new material that does not appear in the companion books.

INTRODUCTION TO SELF-DRIVING CARS

This is a book about self-driving cars. Someday in the future, we'll all have self-driving cars and this book will perhaps seem antiquated, but right now, we are at the forefront of the self-driving car wave. Daily news bombards us with flashes of new announcements by one car maker or another and leaves the impression that within the next few weeks or maybe months that the self-driving car will be here. A casual non-technical reader would assume from these news flashes that in fact we must be on the cusp of a true self-driving car.

Here's a real news flash: We are still quite a distance from having a true self-driving car. It is years to go before we get there.

Why is that? Because a true self-driving car is akin to a moonshot. In the same manner that getting us to the moon was an incredible feat, likewise is achieving a true self-driving car. Anybody that suggests or even brashly states that the true self-driving car is nearly here should be viewed with great skepticism. Indeed, you'll see that I often tend to use the word "hogwash" or "crock" when I assess much of the decidedly ***fake news*** about self-driving cars. Those of us on the inside know that what is often reported to the outside is malarkey. Few of the insiders are willing to say so. I have no such hesitation.

Indeed, I've been writing a popular blog post about self-driving cars and hitting hard on those that try to wave their hands and pretend that we are on the imminent verge of true self-driving cars. For many years, I've been known as the AI Insider. Besides writing about AI, I also develop AI software. I do what I describe. It also gives me insights into what others that are doing AI are really doing versus what it is said they are doing.

Many faithful readers had asked me to pull together my insightful short essays and put them into another book, which you are now holding.

For those of you that have been reading my essays over the years, this collection not only puts them together into one handy package, I also updated the essays and added new material. For those of you that are new to the topic of self-driving cars and AI, I hope you find these essays approachable and informative. I also tend to have a writing style with a bit of a voice, and so you'll see that I am times have a wry sense of humor and poke at conformity.

As a former professor and founder of an AI research lab, I for many years wrote in the formal language of academic writing. I published in referred journals and served as an editor for several AI journals. This writing here is not of the nature, and I have adopted a different and more informal style for these essays. That being said, I also do mention from time-to-time more rigorous material on AI and encourage you all to dig into those deeper and more formal materials if so interested.

I am also an AI practitioner. This means that I write AI software for a living. Currently, I head-up the Cybernetics Self-Driving Car Institute, where we are developing AI software for self-driving cars. I am excited to also report that my son, also a software engineer, heads-up our Cybernetics Self-Driving Car Lab. What I have helped to start, and for which he is an integral part, ultimately he will carry long into the future after I have retired. My daughter, a marketing whiz, also is integral to our efforts as head of our Marketing group. She too will carry forward the legacy now being formulated.

For those of you that are reading this book and have a penchant for writing code, you might consider taking a look at the open source code available for self-driving cars. This is a handy place to start learning how to develop AI for self-driving cars. There are also many new educational courses spring forth. There is a growing body of those wanting to learn about and develop self-driving cars, and a growing body of colleges, labs, and other avenues by which you can learn about self-driving cars.

This book will provide a foundation of aspects that I think will get you ready for those kinds of more advanced training opportunities. If you've already taken those classes, you'll likely find these essays especially interesting as they offer a perspective that I am betting few other instructors or faculty offered to you. These are challenging essays that ask you to think beyond the conventional about self-driving cars.

THE MOTHER OF ALL AI PROJECTS

In June 2017, Apple CEO Tim Cook came out and finally admitted that Apple has been working on a self-driving car. As you'll see in my essays, Apple was enmeshed in secrecy about their self-driving car efforts. We have only been able to read the tea leaves and guess at what Apple has been up to. The notion of an iCar has been floating for quite a while, and self-driving engineers and researchers have been signing tight-lipped Non-Disclosure Agreements (NDA's) to work on projects at Apple that were as shrouded in mystery as any military invasion plans might be.

Tim Cook said something that many others in the Artificial Intelligence (AI) field have been saying, namely, the creation of a self-driving car has got to be the mother of all AI projects. In other words, it is in fact a tremendous moonshot for AI. If a self-driving car can be crafted and the AI works as we hope, it means that we have made incredible strides with AI and that therefore it opens many other worlds of potential breakthrough accomplishments that AI can solve.

Is this hyperbole? Am I just trying to make AI seem like a miracle worker and so provide self-aggrandizing statements for those of us writing the AI software for self-driving cars? No, it is not hyperbole. Developing a true self-driving car is really, really, really hard to do. Let me take a moment to explain why. As a side note, I realize that the Apple CEO is known for at times uttering hyperbole, and he had previously said for example that the year 2012 was "the mother of all years," and he had said that the release of iOS 10 was "the mother of all releases" – all of which does suggest he likes to use the handy "mother of" expression. But, I assure you, in terms of true self-driving cars, he has hit the nail on the head. For sure.

When you think about a moonshot and how we got to the moon, there are some identifiable characteristics and those same aspects can be applied to creating a true self-driving car. You'll notice that I keep putting the word "true" in front of the self-driving car expression. I do so because as per my essay about the various levels of self-driving cars, there are some self-driving cars that are only somewhat of a self-driving car. The somewhat versions are ones that require a human driver to be ready to intervene. In my view, that's not a true self-driving car. A true self-driving car is one that requires no human driver intervention at all. It is a car that can entirely undertake via automation the driving task without any human driver needed. This is the essence of what is known as a Level 5 self-driving car. We are currently at the Level 2 and Level 3 mark, and not yet at Level 5.

Getting to the moon involved aspects such as having big stretch goals, incremental progress, experimentation, innovation, and so on. Let's review how this applied to the moonshot of the bygone era, and how it applies to the self-driving car moonshot of today.

Big Stretch Goal

Trying to take a human and deliver the human to the moon, and bring them back, safely, was an extremely large stretch goal at the time. No one knew whether it could be done. The technology wasn't available yet. The cost was huge. The determination would need to be fierce. Etc. To reach a Level 5 self-driving car is going to be the same. It is a big stretch goal. We can readily get to the Level 3, and we are able to see the Level 4 just up ahead, but a Level 5 is still an unknown as to if it is doable. It should eventually be doable and in the same way that we thought we'd eventually get to the moon, but when it will occur is a different story.

Incremental Progress

Getting to the moon did not happen overnight in one fell swoop. It took years and years of incremental progress to get there. Likewise for self-driving cars. Google has famously been striving to get to the Level 5, and pretty much been willing to forgo dealing with the intervening levels, but most of the other self-driving car makers are doing the incremental route. Let's get a good Level 2 and a somewhat Level 3 going. Then, let's improve the Level 3 and get a somewhat Level 4 going. Then, let's improve the Level 4 and finally arrive at a Level 5. This seems to be the prevalent way that we are going to achieve the true self-driving car.

Experimentation

You likely know that there were various experiments involved in perfecting the approach and technology to get to the moon. As per making incremental progress, we first tried to see if we could get a rocket to go into space and safety return, then put a monkey in there, then with a human, then we went all the way to the moon but didn't land, and finally we arrived at the mission that actually landed on the moon. Self-driving cars are the same way. We are doing simulations of self-driving cars. We do testing of self-driving cars on private land under controlled situations. We do testing of self-driving cars on public roadways, often having to meet regulatory requirements including for example having an engineer or equivalent in the car to take over the controls if needed. And so on. Experiments big and small are needed to figure out what works and what doesn't.

Innovation

There are already some advances in AI that are allowing us to progress toward self-driving cars. We are going to need even more advances. Innovation in all aspects of technology are going to be required to achieve a true self-driving car. By no means do we already have everything in-hand that we need to get there. Expect new inventions and new approaches, new algorithms, etc.

Setbacks

Most of the pundits are avoiding talking about potential setbacks in the progress toward self-driving cars. Getting to the moon involved many setbacks, some of which you never have heard of and were buried at the time so as to not dampen enthusiasm and funding for getting to the moon. A recurring theme in many of my included essays is that there are going to be setbacks as we try to arrive at a true self-driving car. Take a deep breath and be ready. I just hope the setbacks don't completely stop progress. I am sure that it will cause progress to alter in a manner that we've not yet seen in the self-driving car field. I liken the self-driving car of today to the excitement everyone had for Uber when it first got going. Today, we have a different view of Uber and with each passing day there are more regulations to the ride sharing business and more concerns raised. The darling child only stays a darling until finally that child acts up. It will happen the same with self-driving cars.

SELF-DRIVING CARS CHALLENGES

But what exactly makes things so hard to have a true self-driving car, you might be asking. You have seen cruise control for years and years. You've lately seen cars that can do parallel parking. You've seen YouTube videos of Tesla drivers that put their hands out the window as their car zooms along the highway, and seen to therefore be in a self-driving car. Aren't we just needing to put a few more sensors onto a car and then we'll have in-hand a true self-driving car? Nope.

Consider for a moment the nature of the driving task. We don't just let anyone at any age drive a car. Worldwide, most countries won't license a driver until the age of 18, though many do allow a learner's permit at the age of 15 or 16. Some suggest that a younger age would be physically too small to reach the controls of the car. Though this might be the case, we could easily adjust the controls to allow for younger aged and thus smaller stature. It's not their physical size that matters. It's their cognitive development that matters.

To drive a car, you need to be able to reason about the car, what the car can and cannot do. You need to know how to operate the car. You need to know about how other cars on the road drive. You need to know what is allowed in driving such as speed limits and driving within marked lanes. You need to be able to react to situations and be able to avoid getting into accidents. You need to ascertain when to hit your brakes, when to steer clear of a pedestrian, and how to keep from ramming that motorcyclist that just cut you off.

Many of us had taken courses on driving. We studied about driving and took driver training. We had to take a test and pass it to be able to drive. The point being that though most adults take the driving task for granted, and we often "mindlessly" drive our cars, there is a significant amount of cognitive effort that goes into driving a car. After a while, it becomes second nature. You don't especially think about how you drive, you just do it. But, if you watch a novice driver, say a teenager learning to drive, you suddenly realize that there is a lot more complexity to it than we seem to realize.

Furthermore, driving is a very serious task. I recall when my daughter and son first learned to drive. They are both very conscientious people. They wanted to make sure that whatever they did, they did well, and that they did not harm anyone. Every day, when you get into a car, it is probably around 4,000 pounds of hefty metal and plastics (about two tons), and it is a lethal weapon. Think about it. You drive down the street in an object that weighs two tons and with the engine it can accelerate and ram into anything you want to hit. The damage a car can inflict is very scary. Both my children were surprised that they were being given the right to maneuver this monster of a beast that could cause tremendous harm entirely by merely letting go of the steering wheel for a moment or taking your eyes off the road.

In fact, in the United States alone there are about 30,000 deaths per year by auto accidents, which is around 100 per day. Given that there are about 263 million cars in the United States, I am actually more amazed that the number of fatalities is not a lot higher. During my morning commute, I look at all the thousands of cars on the freeway around me, and I think that if all of them decided to go zombie and drive in a crazy maniac way, there would be many people dead. Somehow, incredibly, each day, most people drive relatively safely. To me, that's a miracle right there. Getting millions and millions of people to be safe and sane when behind the wheel of a two ton mobile object, it's a feat that we as a society should admire with pride.

So, hopefully you are in agreement that the driving task requires a great deal of cognition. You don't' need to be especially smart to drive a car, and we've done quite a bit to make car driving viable for even the average dolt. There isn't an IQ test that you need to take to drive a car. If you can read and write, and pass a test, you pretty much can legally drive a car. There are of course some that drive a car and are not legally permitted to do so, plus there are private areas such as farms where drivers are young, but for public roadways in the United States, you can be generally of average intelligence (or less) and be able to legally drive.

This though makes it seem like the cognitive effort must not be much. If the cognitive effort was truly hard, wouldn't we only have Einstein's that could drive a car? We have made sure to keep the driving task as simple as we can, by making the controls easy and relatively standardized, and by having roads that are relatively standardized, and so on. It is as though Disneyland has put their Autopia into the real-world, by us all as a society agreeing that roads will be a certain way, and we'll all abide by the various rules of driving.

A modest cognitive task by a human is still something that stymies AI. You certainly know that AI has been able to beat chess players and be good at other kinds of games. This type of narrow cognition is not what car driving is about. Car driving is much wider. It requires knowledge about the world, which a chess playing AI system does not need to know. The cognitive aspects of driving are on the one hand seemingly simple, but at the same time require layer upon layer of knowledge about cars, people, roads, rules, and a myriad of other "common sense" aspects. We don't have any AI systems today that have that same kind of breadth and depth of awareness and knowledge.

As revealed in my essays, the self-driving car of today is using trickery to do particular tasks. It is all very narrow in operation. Plus, it currently assumes that a human driver is ready to intervene. It is like a child that we have taught to stack blocks, but we are needed to be right there in case the child stacks them too high and they begin to fall over. AI of today is brittle, it is narrow, and it does not approach the cognitive abilities of humans. This is why the true self-driving car is somewhere out in the future.

Another aspect to the driving task is that it is not solely a mind exercise. You do need to use your senses to drive. You use your eyes a vision sensors to see the road ahead. You vision capability is like a streaming video, which your brain needs to continually analyze as you drive. Where is the road? Is there a pedestrian in the way? Is there another car ahead of you? Your senses are relying a flood of info to your brain. Self-driving cars are trying to do the same, by using cameras, radar, ultrasound, and lasers. This is an attempt at mimicking how humans have senses and sensory apparatus.

Thus, the driving task is mental and physical. You use your senses, you use your arms and legs to manipulate the controls of the car, and you use your brain to assess the sensory info and direct your limbs to act upon the controls of the car. This all happens instantly. If you've ever perhaps gotten something in your eye and only had one eye available to drive with, you suddenly realize how dependent upon vision you are. If you have a broken foot with a cast, you suddenly realize how hard it is to control the brake pedal and the accelerator. If you've taken medication and your brain is maybe sluggish, you suddenly realize how much mental strain is required to drive a car.

An AI system that plays chess only needs to be focused on playing chess. The physical aspects aren't important because usually a human moves the chess pieces or the chessboard is shown on an electronic display. Using AI for a more life-and-death task such as analyzing MRI images of patients, this again does not require physical capabilities and instead is done by examining images of bits.

Driving a car is a true life-and-death task. It is a use of AI that can easily and at any moment produce death. For those colleagues of mine that are developing this AI, as am I, we need to keep in mind the somber aspects of this. We are producing software that will have in its virtual hands the lives of the occupants of the car, and the lives of those in other nearby cars, and the lives of nearby pedestrians, etc. Chess is not usually a life-or-death matter.

Driving is all around us. Cars are everywhere. Most of today's AI applications involve only a small number of people. Or, they are behind the scenes and we as humans have other recourse if the AI messes up. AI that is driving a car at 80 miles per hour on a highway had better not mess up. The consequences are grave. Multiply this by the number of cars, if we could put magically self-driving into every car in the USA, we'd have AI running in the 263 million cars. That's a lot of AI spread around. This is AI on a massive scale that we are not doing today and that offers both promise and potential peril.

There are some that want AI for self-driving cars because they envision a world without any car accidents. They envision a world in which there is no car congestion and all cars cooperate with each other. These are wonderful utopian visions.

They are also very misleading. The adoption of self-driving cars is going to be incremental and not overnight. We cannot economically just junk all existing cars. Nor are we going to be able to affordably retrofit existing cars. It is more likely that self-driving cars will be built into new cars and that over many years of gradual replacement of existing cars that we'll see the mix of self-driving cars become substantial in the real-world.

In these essays, I have tried to offer technological insights without being overly technical in my description, and also blended the business, societal, and economic aspects too. Technologists need to consider the non-technological impacts of what they do. Non-technologists should be aware of what is being developed.

We all need to work together to collectively be prepared for the enormous disruption and transformative aspects of true self-driving cars. We all need to be involved in this mother of all AI projects.

WHAT THIS BOOK PROVIDES

What does this book provide to you? It introduces many of the key elements about self-driving cars and does so with an AI based perspective. I weave together technical and non-technical aspects, readily going from being concerned about the cognitive capabilities of the driving task and how the technology is embodying this into self-driving cars, and in the next breath I discuss the societal and economic aspects.

They are all intertwined because that's the way reality is. You cannot separate out the technology per se, and instead must consider it within the milieu of what is being invented and innovated, and do so with a mindset towards the contemporary mores and culture that shape what we are doing and what we hope to do.

WHY THIS BOOK

I wrote this book to try and bring to the public view many aspects about self-driving cars that nobody seems to be discussing.

For business leaders that are either involved in making self-driving cars or that are going to leverage self-driving cars, I hope that this book will enlighten you as to the risks involved and ways in which you should be strategizing about how to deal with those risks.

For entrepreneurs, startups and other businesses that want to enter into the self-driving car market that is emerging, I hope this book sparks your interest in doing so, and provides some sense of what might be prudent to pursue.

For researchers that study self-driving cars, I hope this book spurs your interest in the risks and safety issues of self-driving cars, and also nudges you toward conducting research on those aspects.

For students in computer science or related disciplines, I hope this book will provide you with interesting and new ideas and material, for which you might conduct research or provide some career direction insights for you.

For AI companies and high-tech companies pursuing self-driving cars, this book will hopefully broaden your view beyond just the mere coding and development needed to make self-driving cars.

For all readers, I hope that you will find the material in this book to be stimulating. Some of it will be repetitive of things you already know. But I am pretty sure that you'll also find various eureka moments whereby you'll discover a new technique or approach that you had not earlier thought of. I am also betting that there will be material that forces you to rethink some of your current practices.

I am not saying you will suddenly have an epiphany and change what you are doing. I do think though that you will reconsider or perhaps revisit what you are doing.

For anyone choosing to use this book for teaching purposes, please take a look at my suggestions for doing so, as described in the Appendix. I have found the material handy in courses that I have taught, and likewise other faculty have told me that they have found the material handy, in some cases as extended readings and in other instances as a core part of their course (depending on the nature of the class).

In my writing for this book, I have tried carefully to blend both the practitioner and the academic styles of writing. It is not as dense as is typical academic journal writing, but at the same time offers depth by going into the nuances and trade-offs of various practices.

The word "deep" is in vogue today, meaning getting deeply into a subject or topic, and so is the word "unpack" which means to tease out the underlying aspects of a subject or topic. I have sought to offer material that addresses an issue or topic by going relatively deeply into it and make sure that it is well unpacked.

Finally, in any book about AI, it is difficult to use our everyday words without having some of them be misinterpreted. Specifically, it is easy to anthropomorphize AI. When I say that an AI system "knows" something, I do not want you to construe that the AI system has sentience and "knows" in the same way that humans do. They aren't that way, as yet. I have tried to use quotes around such words from time-to-time to emphasize that the words I am using should not be misinterpreted to ascribe true human intelligence to the AI systems that we know of today. If I used quotes around all such words, the book would be very difficult to read, and so I am doing so judiciously. Please keep that in mind as you read the material, thanks.

COMPANION BOOKS

If you find this material of interest, you might enjoy these too:

1. **"Introduction to Driverless Self-Driving Cars"** by Dr. Lance Eliot
2. **"Innovation and Thought Leadership on Self-Driving Driverless Cars"** by Dr. Lance Eliot
3. **"Advances in AI and Autonomous Vehicles: Cybernetic Self-Driving Cars"** by Dr. Lance Eliot
4. **"Self-Driving Cars: The Mother of All AI Projects"** by Dr. Lance Eliot
5. **"New Advances in AI Autonomous Driverless Self-Driving Cars"** by Dr. Lance Eliot
6. **"Autonomous Vehicle Driverless Self-Driving Cars and Artificial Intelligence"** by Dr. Lance Eliot and Michael B. Eliot
7. **"Transformative Artificial Intelligence Driverless Self-Driving Cars"** by Dr. Lance Eliot
8. **"Disruptive Artificial Intelligence and Driverless Self-Driving Cars"** by Dr. Lance Eliot
9. "**State-of-the-Art AI Driverless Self-Driving Cars**" by Dr. Lance Eliot
10. "**Top Trends in AI Self-Driving Cars**" by Dr. Lance Eliot
11. **"AI Innovations and Self-Driving Cars"** by Dr. Lance Eliot
12. **"Crucial Advances for AI Driverless Cars"** by Dr. Lance Eliot
13. **"Sociotechnical Insights and AI Driverless Cars**" by Dr. Lance Eliot.
14. **"Pioneering Advances for AI Driverless Cars"** by Dr. Lance Eliot
15. **"Leading Edge Trends for AI Driverless Cars"** by Dr. Lance Eliot
16. **"The Cutting Edge of AI Autonomous Cars"** by Dr. Lance Eliot
17. **"The Next Wave of AI Self-Driving Cars"** by Dr. Lance Eliot
18. **"Revolutionary Innovations of AI Driverless Cars"** by Dr. Lance Eliot
19. **"AI Self-Driving Cars Breakthroughs"** by Dr. Lance Eliot
20. **"Trailblazing Trends for AI Self-Driving Cars"** by Dr. Lance Eliot
21. **"Ingenious Strides for AI Driverless Cars"** by Dr. Lance Eliot
22. **"AI Self-Driving Cars Inventiveness"** by Dr. Lance Eliot
23. **"Visionary Secrets of AI Driverless Cars"** by Dr. Lance Eliot
24. **"Spearheading AI Self-Driving Cars"** by Dr. Lance Eliot
25. **"Spurring AI Self-Driving Cars"** by Dr. Lance Eliot
26. **"Avant-Garde AI Driverless Cars"** by Dr. Lance Eliot
27. **"AI Self-Driving Cars Evolvement"** by Dr. Lance Eliot

These books are available on Amazon and at other major global booksellers.

CHAPTER 1

ELIOT FRAMEWORK FOR AI SELF-DRIVING CARS

CHAPTER 1
ELIOT FRAMEWORK FOR AI SELF-DRIVING CARS

This chapter is a core foundational aspect for understanding AI self-driving cars and I have used this same chapter in several of my other books to introduce the reader to essential elements of this field. Once you've read this chapter, you'll be prepared to read the rest of the material since the foundational essence of the components of autonomous AI driverless self-driving cars will have been established for you.

When I give presentations about self-driving cars and teach classes on the topic, I have found it helpful to provide a framework around which the various key elements of self-driving cars can be understood and organized (see diagram at the end of this chapter). The framework needs to be simple enough to convey the overarching elements, but at the same time not so simple that it belies the true complexity of self-driving cars. As such, I am going to describe the framework here and try to offer in a thousand words (or more!) what the framework diagram itself intends to portray.

The core elements on the diagram are numbered for ease of reference. The numbering does not suggest any kind of prioritization of the elements. Each element is crucial. Each element has a purpose, and otherwise would not be included in the framework. For some self-driving cars, a particular element might be more important or somehow distinguished in comparison to other self-driving cars.

You could even use the framework to rate a particular self-driving car, doing so by gauging how well it performs in each of the elements of the framework. I will describe each of the elements, one at a time. After doing so, I'll discuss aspects that illustrate how the elements interact and perform during the overall effort of a self-driving car.

At the Cybernetic Self-Driving Car Institute, we use the framework to keep track of what we are working on, and how we are developing software that fills in what is needed to achieve Level 5 self-driving cars.

D-01: Sensor Capture

Let's start with the one element that often gets the most attention in the press about self-driving cars, namely, the sensory devices for a self-driving car.

On the framework, the box labeled as D-01 indicates "Sensor Capture" and refers to the processes of the self-driving car that involve collecting data from the myriad of sensors that are used for a self-driving car. The types of devices typically involved are listed, such as the use of mono cameras, stereo cameras, LIDAR devices, radar systems, ultrasonic devices, GPS, IMU, and so on.

These devices are tasked with obtaining data about the status of the self-driving car and the world around it. Some of the devices are continually providing updates, while others of the devices await an indication by the self-driving car that the device is supposed to collect data. The data might be first transformed in some fashion by the device itself, or it might instead be fed directly into the sensor capture as raw data. At that point, it might be up to the sensor capture processes to do transformations on the data. This all varies depending upon the nature of the devices being used and how the devices were designed and developed.

D-02: Sensor Fusion

Imagine that your eyeballs receive visual images, your nose receives odors, your ears receive sounds, and in essence each of your distinct sensory devices is getting some form of input. The input befits the nature of the device. Likewise, for a self-driving car, the cameras provide visual images, the radar returns radar reflections, and so on.

Each device provides the data as befits what the device does.

At some point, using the analogy to humans, you need to merge together what your eyes see, what your nose smells, what your ears hear, and piece it all together into a larger sense of what the world is all about and what is happening around you. Sensor fusion is the action of taking the singular aspects from each of the devices and putting them together into a larger puzzle.

Sensor fusion is a tough task. There are some devices that might not be working at the time of the sensor capture. Or, there might some devices that are unable to report well what they have detected. Again, using a human analogy, suppose you are in a dark room and so your eyes cannot see much. At that point, you might need to rely more so on your ears and what you hear. The same is true for a self-driving car. If the cameras are obscured due to snow and sleet, it might be that the radar can provide a greater indication of what the external conditions consist of.

In the case of a self-driving car, there can be a plethora of such sensory devices. Each is reporting what it can. Each might have its difficulties. Each might have its limitations, such as how far ahead it can detect an object. All of these limitations need to be considered during the sensor fusion task.

D-03: Virtual World Model

For humans, we presumably keep in our minds a model of the world around us when we are driving a car. In your mind, you know that the car is going at say 60 miles per hour and that you are on a freeway. You have a model in your mind that your car is surrounded by other cars, and that there are lanes to the freeway. Your model is not only based on what you can see, hear, etc., but also what you know about the nature of the world. You know that at any moment that car ahead of you can smash on its brakes, or the car behind you can ram into your car, or that the truck in the next lane might swerve into your lane.

The AI of the self-driving car needs to have a virtual world model, which it then keeps updated with whatever it is receiving from the sensor fusion, which received its input from the sensor capture and the sensory devices.

D-04: System Action Plan

By having a virtual world model, the AI of the self-driving car is able to keep track of where the car is and what is happening around the car. In addition, the AI needs to determine what to do next. Should the self-driving car hit its brakes? Should the self-driving car stay in its lane or swerve into the lane to the left? Should the self-driving car accelerate or slow down?

A system action plan needs to be prepared by the AI of the self-driving car. The action plan specifies what actions should be taken. The actions need to pertain to the status of the virtual world model. Plus, the actions need to be realizable.

This realizability means that the AI cannot just assert that the self-driving car should suddenly sprout wings and fly. Instead, the AI must be bound by whatever the self-driving car can actually do, such as coming to a halt in a distance of X feet at a speed of Y miles per hour, rather than perhaps asserting that the self-driving car come to a halt in 0 feet as though it could instantaneously come to a stop while it is in motion.

D-05: Controls Activation

The system action plan is implemented by activating the controls of the car to act according to what the plan stipulates. This might mean that the accelerator control is commanded to increase the speed of the car. Or, the steering control is commanded to turn the steering wheel 30 degrees to the left or right.

One question arises as to whether or not the controls respond as they are commanded to do. In other words, suppose the AI has commanded the accelerator to increase, but for some reason it does not do so. Or, maybe it tries to do so, but the speed of the car does not increase. The controls activation feeds back into the virtual world model, and simultaneously the virtual world model is getting updated from the sensors, the sensor capture, and the sensor fusion. This allows the AI to ascertain what has taken place as a result of the controls being commanded to take some kind of action.

By the way, please keep in mind that though the diagram seems to have a linear progression to it, the reality is that these are all aspects of the self-driving car that are happening in parallel and simultaneously. The sensors are capturing data, meanwhile the sensor fusion is taking place, meanwhile the virtual model is being updated, meanwhile the system action plan is being formulated and reformulated, meanwhile the controls are being activated.

This is the same as a human being that is driving a car. They are eyeballing the road, meanwhile they are fusing in their mind the sights, sounds, etc., meanwhile their mind is updating their model of the world around them, meanwhile they are formulating an action plan of what to do, and meanwhile they are pushing their foot onto the pedals and steering the car. In the normal course of driving a car, you are doing all of these at once. I mention this so that when you look at the diagram, you will think of the boxes as processes that are all happening at the same time, and not as though only one happens and then the next.

They are shown diagrammatically in a simplistic manner to help comprehend what is taking place. You though should also realize that they are working in parallel and simultaneous with each other. This is a tough aspect in that the inter-element communications involve latency and other aspects that must be taken into account. There can be delays in one element updating and then sharing its latest status with other elements.

D-06: Automobile & CAN

Contemporary cars use various automotive electronics and a Controller Area Network (CAN) to serve as the components that underlie the driving aspects of a car. There are Electronic Control Units (ECU's) which control subsystems of the car, such as the engine, the brakes, the doors, the windows, and so on.

The elements D-01, D-02, D-03, D-04, D-05 are layered on top of the D-06, and must be aware of the nature of what the D-06 is able to do and not do.

D-07: In-Car Commands

Humans are going to be occupants in self-driving cars. In a Level 5 self-driving car, there must be some form of communication that takes place between the humans and the self-driving car. For example, I go into a self-driving car and tell it that I want to be driven over to Disneyland, and along the way I want to stop at In-and-Out Burger. The self-driving car now parses what I've said and tries to then establish a means to carry out my wishes.

In-car commands can happen at any time during a driving journey. Though my example was about an in-car command when I first got into my self-driving car, it could be that while the self-driving car is carrying out the journey that I change my mind. Perhaps after getting stuck in traffic, I tell the self-driving car to forget about getting the burgers and just head straight over to the theme park. The self-driving car needs to be alert to in-car commands throughout the journey.

D-08: V2X Communications

We will ultimately have self-driving cars communicating with each other, doing so via V2V (Vehicle-to-Vehicle) communications. We will also have self-driving cars that communicate with the roadways and other aspects of the transportation infrastructure, doing so via V2I (Vehicle-to-Infrastructure).

The variety of ways in which a self-driving car will be communicating with other cars and infrastructure is being called V2X, whereby the letter X means whatever else we identify as something that a car should or would want to communicate with. The V2X communications will be taking place simultaneous with everything else on the diagram, and those other elements will need to incorporate whatever it gleans from those V2X communications.

D-09: Deep Learning

The use of Deep Learning permeates all other aspects of the self-driving car. The AI of the self-driving car will be using deep learning to do a better job at the systems action plan, and at the controls activation, and at the sensor fusion, and so on.

Currently, the use of artificial neural networks is the most prevalent form of deep learning. Based on large swaths of data, the neural networks attempt to "learn" from the data and therefore direct the efforts of the self-driving car accordingly.

D-10: Tactical AI

Tactical AI is the element of dealing with the moment-to-moment driving of the self-driving car. Is the self-driving car staying in its lane of the freeway? Is the car responding appropriately to the controls commands? Are the sensory devices working?

For human drivers, the tactical equivalent can be seen when you watch a novice driver such as a teenager that is first driving. They are focused on the mechanics of the driving task, keeping their eye on the road while also trying to properly control the car.

D-11: Strategic AI

The Strategic AI aspects of a self-driving car are dealing with the larger picture of what the self-driving car is trying to do. If I had asked that the self-driving car take me to Disneyland, there is an overall journey map that needs to be kept and maintained.

There is an interaction between the Strategic AI and the Tactical AI. The Strategic AI is wanting to keep on the mission of the driving, while the Tactical AI is focused on the particulars underway in the driving effort. If the Tactical AI seems to wander away from the overarching mission, the Strategic AI wants to see why and get things back on track. If the Tactical AI realizes that there is something amiss on the self-driving car, it needs to alert the Strategic AI accordingly and have an adjustment to the overarching mission that is underway.

D-12: Self-Aware AI

Very few of the self-driving cars being developed are including a Self-Aware AI element, which we at the Cybernetic Self-Driving Car Institute believe is crucial to Level 5 self-driving cars.

The Self-Aware AI element is intended to watch over itself, in the sense that the AI is making sure that the AI is working as intended. Suppose you had a human driving a car, and they were starting to drive erratically. Hopefully, their own self-awareness would make them realize they themselves are driving poorly, such as perhaps starting to fall asleep after having been driving for hours on end. If you had a passenger in the car, they might be able to alert the driver if the driver is starting to do something amiss. This is exactly what the Self-Aware

AI element tries to do, it becomes the overseer of the AI, and tries to detect when the AI has become faulty or confused, and then find ways to overcome the issue.

D-13: Economic

The economic aspects of a self-driving car are not per se a technology aspect of a self-driving car, but the economics do indeed impact the nature of a self-driving car. For example, the cost of outfitting a self-driving car with every kind of possible sensory device is prohibitive, and so choices need to be made about which devices are used. And, for those sensory devices chosen, whether they would have a full set of features or a more limited set of features.

We are going to have self-driving cars that are at the low-end of a consumer cost point, and others at the high-end of a consumer cost point. You cannot expect that the self-driving car at the low-end is going to be as robust as the one at the high-end. I realize that many of the self-driving car pundits are acting as though all self-driving cars will be the same, but they won't be. Just like anything else, we are going to have self-driving cars that have a range of capabilities. Some will be better than others. Some will be safer than others. This is the way of the real-world, and so we need to be thinking about the economics aspects when considering the nature of self-driving cars.

D-14: Societal

This component encompasses the societal aspects of AI which also impacts the technology of self-driving cars. For example, the famous Trolley Problem involves what choices should a self-driving car make when faced with life-and-death matters. If the self-driving car is about to either hit a child standing in the roadway, or instead ram into a tree at the side of the road and possibly kill the humans in the self-driving car, which choice should be made?

We need to keep in mind the societal aspects will underlie the AI of the self-driving car. Whether we are aware of it explicitly or not, the AI will have embedded into it various societal assumptions.

D-15: Innovation

I included the notion of innovation into the framework because we can anticipate that whatever a self-driving car consists of, it will continue to be innovated over time. The self-driving cars coming out in the next several years will undoubtedly be different and less innovative than the versions that come out in ten years hence, and so on.

Framework Overall

For those of you that want to learn about self-driving cars, you can potentially pick a particular element and become specialized in that aspect. Some engineers are focusing on the sensory devices. Some engineers focus on the controls activation. And so on. There are specialties in each of the elements.

Researchers are likewise specializing in various aspects. For example, there are researchers that are using Deep Learning to see how best it can be used for sensor fusion. There are other researchers that are using Deep Learning to derive good System Action Plans. Some are studying how to develop AI for the Strategic aspects of the driving task, while others are focused on the Tactical aspects.

A well-prepared all-around software developer that is involved in self-driving cars should be familiar with all of the elements, at least to the degree that they know what each element does. This is important since whatever piece of the pie that the software developer works on, they need to be knowledgeable about what the other elements are doing.

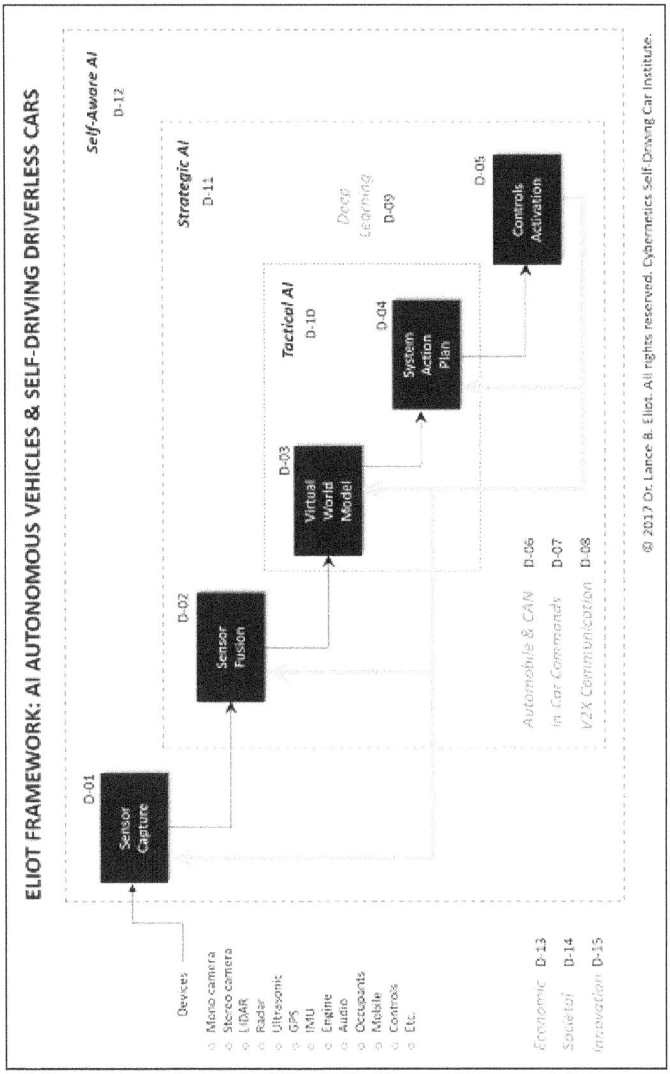
ELIOT FRAMEWORK: AI AUTONOMOUS VEHICLES & SELF-DRIVING DRIVERLESS CARS
Self-Aware AI
D-12
Strategic AI
D-11
Tactical AI
D-10
Deep Learning
D-09
D-01
Sensor Capture
D-02
Sensor Fusion
D-03
Virtual World Model
D-04
System Action Plan
D-05
Controls Activation
Automobile & CAN D-06
In-Car Commands D-07
V2X Communication D-08
Devices
Mono camera
Stereo camera
LIDAR
Radar
Ultrasonic
GPS
IMU
Engine
Audio
Occupants
Mobile
Controls
Etc.
Economic D-13
Societal D-14
Innovation D-15
© 2017 Dr. Lance B. Eliot. All rights reserved. Cybernetics Self-Driving Car Institute.

CHAPTER 2

CHIEF SAFETY OFFICERS AND AI SELF-DRIVING CARS

CHAPTER 2

CHIEF SAFETY OFFICERS AND AI SELF-DRIVING CARS

Many firms think of a Chief Safety Officer (CSO) in a somewhat narrow manner as someone that deals with in-house occupational health and safety aspects occurring solely in the workplace. Though adherence to proper safety matters within a company are certainly paramount, there is an even larger role for CSO's that has been sparked by the advent of Artificial Intelligence (AI) systems. Emerging AI systems that are being embedded into a company's products and services has stoked the realization that a new kind of Chief Safety Officer is needed, one with wider duties and requiring a dual internal/external persona and focus.

In some cases, especially life-or-death kinds of AI-based products such as AI self-driving cars, it is crucial that there be a Chief Safety Officer at the highest levels of a company. The CSO needs to be provided with the kind of breadth and depth of capability required to carry out their now fuller charge. By being at or within the top executive leadership, they can aid in shaping the design, development, and fielding of these crucial life-determining AI systems.

Gradually, auto makers and tech firms in the AI self-driving car realm are bringing on-board a Chief Safety Officer or equivalent. It's not happening fast enough, I assert, yet at least it is a promising trend and one that needs to speed along.

Without a prominent position of Chief Safety Officer, it is doubtful that auto makers and tech firms will give the requisite attention and due care toward safety of AI self-driving cars.

I worry too that those firms not putting in place an appropriate Chief Safety Officer are risking not only the lives of those that will use their AI self-driving cars, but also putting into jeopardy the advent of AI self-driving cars all told.

In essence, those firms that give lip service to safety of AI self-driving car systems or inadvertently fail to provide the upmost attention to safety, they are likely to bring forth adverse safety events on our roadways, and for which the public and regulators will react not just toward that offending firm, such incidents will become an outcry and overarching barrier to any furtherance of AI self-driving cars.

Simply stated, for AI self-driving cars, the chances of a bad apple spoiling the barrel is quite high and something that all of us in this industry live on the edge of each day.

In speaking with Mark Rosekind, Chief Safety Innovation Officer at Zoox, doing so at a recent Autonomous Vehicle event in Silicon Valley, he emphasized how safety considerations are vital in the AI self-driving car arena. His years as an administrator for the National Highway Traffic Safety Administration (NHTSA) and his service on the board of the National Transportation Safety Board (NTSB) provide a quite on-target skillset and base of experience for his role. For those of you interested in the overall approach to safety that Zoox is pursuing, you can take a look at their posted report: https://zoox.com/safety/

Those of you that follow closely my postings will remember that I had previously mentioned the efforts of Chris Hart in the safety aspects of AI self-driving cars. As a former chairman of the NTSB, he brings key insights to what the auto makers and tech firms need to be doing about safety, along with offering important views that can help shape regulations and regulatory actions (see his web site: https://hartsolutionsllc.com/).

You might find of interest his recent blog post about the differences between aviation automation and AI self-driving cars, which dovetails too into my viewpoint about the same topic. For Chris Hart's recent blog post, see: http://www.thedrive.com/tech/26896/self-driving-safety-steps-into-the-unknown

Waymo, Google/Alphabet's entity well-known for its prominence in the AI self-driving car industry, has also brought on-board a Chief Safety Officer, namely Debbie Hersman. Besides her having served on the NTSB and having been its chairman, she also was the CEO and President of the National Safety Council. It was with welcome relief that she has come on-board to Waymo since it also sends a signal or sign to the rest of the AI self-driving car makers that this is a crucial role and one they too need to make sure they are embracing if they aren't already doing so.

Uber recently brought on-board Nat Beuse to head their safety efforts. He had been with the U.S. Department of Transportation and oversaw vehicle safety efforts there for many years. For those of you interested in the safety report that Uber produced last year, coming after their internal review of the Uber self-driving car incident, you can find the report posted here: https://www.uber.com/info/atg/safety/

I'd also like to mention the efforts of Alex Epstein, Director of Transportation at the National Safety Council (NSC). We met at an inaugural conference on the safety of AI self-driving cars and his insights and remarks were spot-on about where the industry is and where it needs to go. At the NSC he is leading their Advanced Automotive Safety Technology initiative. His efforts of public outreach are notable and the public campaign of MyCarDoesWhat is an example of how we need to aid the public in understanding the facets of car automation: https://mycardoeswhat.org/

Defining the Chief Safety Officer Role

I have found it useful to clarify what I mean by the role of a Chief Safety Officer in the context of a firm that has an AI-based product or service, particularly such as the AI self-driving car industry.

As shown, the Chief Safety Officer has a number of important role elements. These elements all intertwine with each other and should not be construed as independent of each other. They are an integrated mesh of the space of safety elements needed to be fostered and led by the Chief Safety Officer. Allowing one of the elements to languish or be undervalued is likely to undermine the integrity of any safety related programs or approaches undertaken by a firm.

The nine core elements for a Chief Safety Officer consist of:

- Safety Strategy
- Safety Company Culture
- Safety Policies
- Safety Education
- Safety Awareness
- Safety External
- Safety SDLC
- Safety Reporting
- Safety Crisis Management

I'll next describe each of the elements.

I'm going to focus on the AI self-driving car industry, but you can hopefully see how these can be applied to other areas of AI that involve safety-related AI-based products or services. Perhaps you make AI-based robots that will be working in warehouses or factories, etc., which these elements would then pertain to equally.

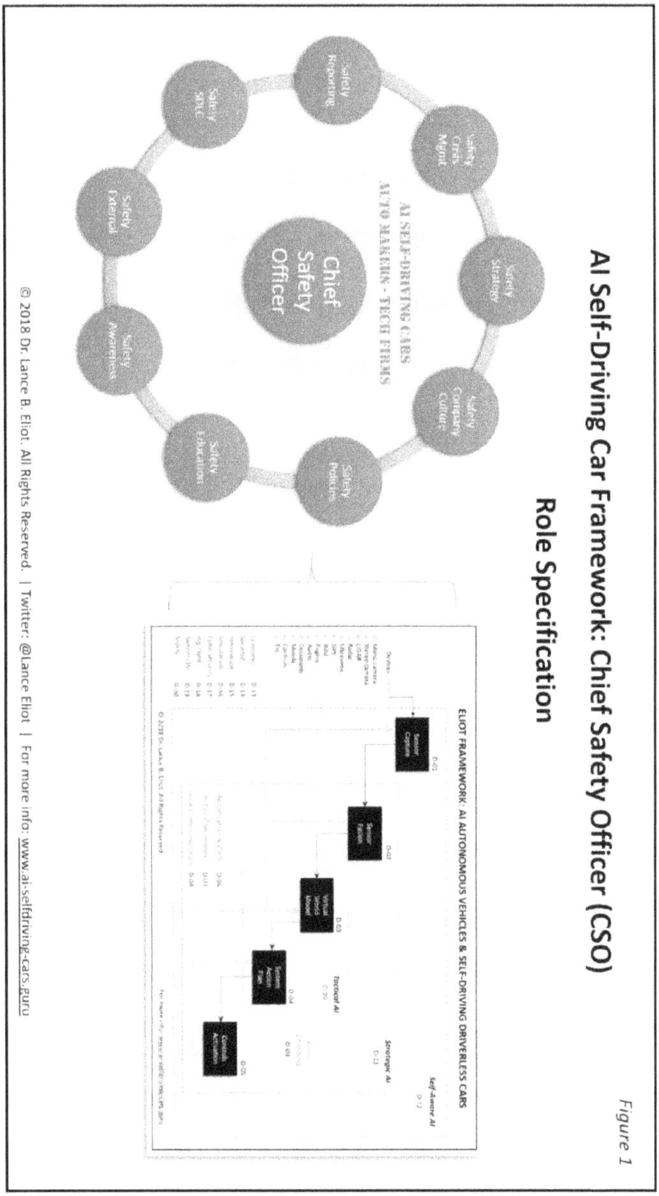
AI Self-Driving Car Framework: Chief Safety Officer (CSO)
Role Specification
Figure 1
Chief Safety Officer
AI SELF-DRIVING CARS
AUTO MAKERS - TECH FIRMS
Safety Strategy
Safety Company Culture
Safety Policies
Safety Education
Safety Awareness
Safety External
Safety SDLC
Safety Reporting
Safety Crisis Mgmt
ELIOT FRAMEWORK: AI AUTONOMOUS VEHICLES & SELF-DRIVING DRIVERLESS CARS
© 2018 Dr. Lance B. Eliot. All Rights Reserved. | Twitter: @Lance Eliot | For more info: www.ai-selfdriving-cars.guru

I am also going to omit the other kinds of non-AI safety matters that the Chief Safety Officer would likely encompass, which are well documented already in numerous online Chief Safety Officer descriptions and specifications.

Here's a brief indication about each element.

- **Safety Strategy**

The Chief Safety Officer establishes the overall strategy of how safety will be incorporated into the AI systems and works hand-in-hand with the other top executives in doing so. This must be done collaboratively since the rest of the executive team must "buy into" the safety strategy and be willing and able to carry it out. Safety is not an island of itself. Each of the functions of the firm must have a stake in and will be required to ensure the safety strategy is being implemented.

- **Safety Company Culture**

The Chief Safety Officer needs to help shape the culture of the company to be on a safety-first mindset. Often times, AI developers and other tech personal are not versed in safety and might have come from a university setting wherein AI systems were done as prototypes, and safety was not a particular pressing topic.

Some will even potentially believe that "safety is the enemy of innovation," which is at times a rampant false belief. The company culture might require some heavy lifting and has to be done in conjunction with the top leadership team and done in a meaningful way rather than a light-hearted or surface-level manner.

- **Safety Policies**

The Chief Safety Officer should put together a set of safety policies indicating how the AI systems need to be conceived of, designed, built, tested, and fielded to embody key principles of safety.

These policies need to be readily comprehensible and there needs to a clear-cut means to abide by the policies. If the policies are overly abstract or obtuse, or if they are impractical, it will likely foster a sense of "it's just CYA" and the rest of the firm will tend to disregard the policies.

- **Safety Education**

The Chief Safety Officer should identify the kinds of educational means that can be made available throughout the firm to increase an understanding of what safety means in the context of developing and fielding AI systems.

This can be a combination of internally prepared AI safety classes and externally provided ones. The top executives should also participate in the educational programs to showcase their belief in and support for the educational aspects, and they should work with the Chief Safety Officer in scheduling and ensuring that the teams and staff undertake the classes, along with follow-up to ascertain that the education is being put into active use.

- **Safety Awareness**

The Chief Safety Officer should undertake to have safety awareness become an ongoing activity, often fostered by posting AI safety related aspects on the corporate Intranet, along with providing other avenues in which AI safety is discussed and encouraged such as brown bag lunch sessions, sharing of AI safety tips and suggestions from within the firm, and so on.

This needs to be an ongoing effort and not allow a one-time push of safety that then decays or becomes forgotten.

- **Safety External**

The Chief Safety Officer should be proactive in representing the company and its AI safety efforts to external stakeholders. This includes doing so with regulators, possibly participating in regulatory efforts or reviews when appropriate, along with speaking at industry events about the safety related work being undertaken and conferring with the media.

As the external face of the company, the CSO will also likely get feedback from the external stakeholders, which then should be refed into the company and be especially discussed with the top leadership team.

- **Safety SDLC**

The Chief Safety Officer should help ensure that the Systems Development Life Cycle (SDLC) includes safety throughout each of the stages.

This includes whether the SDLC is agile-oriented or waterfall or in whatever method or manner being undertaken. Checkpoints and reviews need to include the safety aspects and have teeth, meaning that if safety is either not being included or being shortchanged, this becomes an effort stopping criteria that cannot be swept under the rug. It is easy during the pressures of development to shove aside safety portions and coding, under the guise of "getting on with the real coding," but that's not going to cut it in AI systems involving life-or-death systems consequences.

- **Safety Reporting**

The Chief Safety Officer needs to put in place a means to keep track of safety aspects that are being considered and included into the AI systems. This is typically an online tracking and reporting system. Out of the tracking system, reporting needs to be made available on an ongoing basis.

This includes dashboards and flash reporting, which is vital since if the reporting is overly delayed or difficult to obtain or interpret, it will be considered "too late to deal with" and the cost or effort to make safety related corrections or additions will be subordinated.

- **Safety Crisis Management**

The Chief Safety Officer should establish a crisis management approach to deal with any AI safety related faults or issues that arise. Firms often seem to scramble when their AI self-driving car has injured someone, yet this is something that could have been anticipated as a possibility, and preparations could have been made beforehand.

The response to an AI safety adverse act needs to be carefully coordinated and the company will likely be seen as either doing sincere efforts about the incident or if ill-prepared might make matters untoward and undermine the company efforts and those of other AI self-driving car makers.

In Figure 1, I've also included my framework of AI self-driving cars.

Each of the nine elements that I've just described can be applied to each of the aspects of the framework. For example, how is safety being included into the sensors design, development, testing, and fielding? How is safety being included into the sensor fusion design, development, testing, and fielding? How is safety being included into the virtual world model design, development, testing, and fielding.

You are unlikely to have many safety related considerations in say the sensors if there isn't an overarching belief at the firm that safety is important, which is showcased by having a Chief Safety Officer, and by having a company culture that embraces safety, and by educating the teams that are doing the development about AI safety, etc. This highlights my earlier point that each of the elements must work as an integrative whole.

Suppose the firm actually does eight of the elements but doesn't do anything about how to incorporate AI safety into the SDLC. What then?

This means that the AI developers are left to their own to try and devise how to incorporate safety into their development efforts. They might fumble around doing so, or take bona fide stabs at it, though it is fragmented and disconnected from the rest of the development methodology.

Furthermore, worse still, the odds are that the SDLC has no place particularly for safety, which means no metrics about safety, and therefore the pressure to not do anything related to safety is enhanced, due to the metrics measuring the AI developers in other ways that don't necessarily have much to do with safety. The point being that each of the nine elements need to work collectively.

Resources on Baking AI Safety Into AI Self-Driving Car Efforts

At the Cybernetic AI Self-Driving Car Institute, we are developing AI software for self-driving cars. We consider AI safety aspects as essential to our efforts and urge auto makers and tech firms to do likewise.

I'd like to first clarify and introduce the notion that there are varying levels of AI self-driving cars. The topmost level is considered Level 5. A Level 5 self-driving car is one that is being driven by the AI and there is no human driver involved. For the design of Level 5 self-driving cars, the auto makers are even removing the gas pedal, brake pedal, and steering wheel, since those are contraptions used by human drivers. The Level 5 self-driving car is not being driven by a human and nor is there an expectation that a human driver will be present in the self-driving car. It's all on the shoulders of the AI to drive the car.

For self-driving cars less than a Level 5, there must be a human driver present in the car. The human driver is currently considered the responsible party for the acts of the car. The AI and the human driver are co-sharing the driving task.

In spite of this co-sharing, the human is supposed to remain fully immersed into the driving task and be ready at all times to perform the driving task. I've repeatedly warned about the dangers of this co-sharing arrangement and predicted it will produce many untoward results.

Let's focus herein on the true Level 5 self-driving car. Much of the comments apply to the less than Level 5 self-driving cars too, but the fully autonomous AI self-driving car will receive the most attention in this discussion.

Here's the usual steps involved in the AI driving task:

- Sensor data collection and interpretation
- Sensor fusion
- Virtual world model updating
- AI action planning
- Car controls command issuance

Another key aspect of AI self-driving cars is that they will be driving on our roadways in the midst of human driven cars too. There are some pundits of AI self-driving cars that continually refer to a utopian world in which there are only AI self-driving cars on the public roads. Currently there are about 250+ million conventional cars in the United States alone, and those cars are not going to magically disappear or become true Level 5 AI self-driving cars overnight.

Indeed, the use of human driven cars will last for many years, likely many decades, and the advent of AI self-driving cars will occur while there are still human driven cars on the roads. This is a crucial point since this means that the AI of self-driving cars needs to be able to contend with not just other AI self-driving cars, but also contend with human driven cars. It is easy to envision a simplistic and rather unrealistic world in which all AI self-driving cars are politely interacting with each other and being civil about roadway interactions. That's not what is going to be happening for the foreseeable future. AI self-driving cars and human driven cars will need to be able to cope with each other. Period.

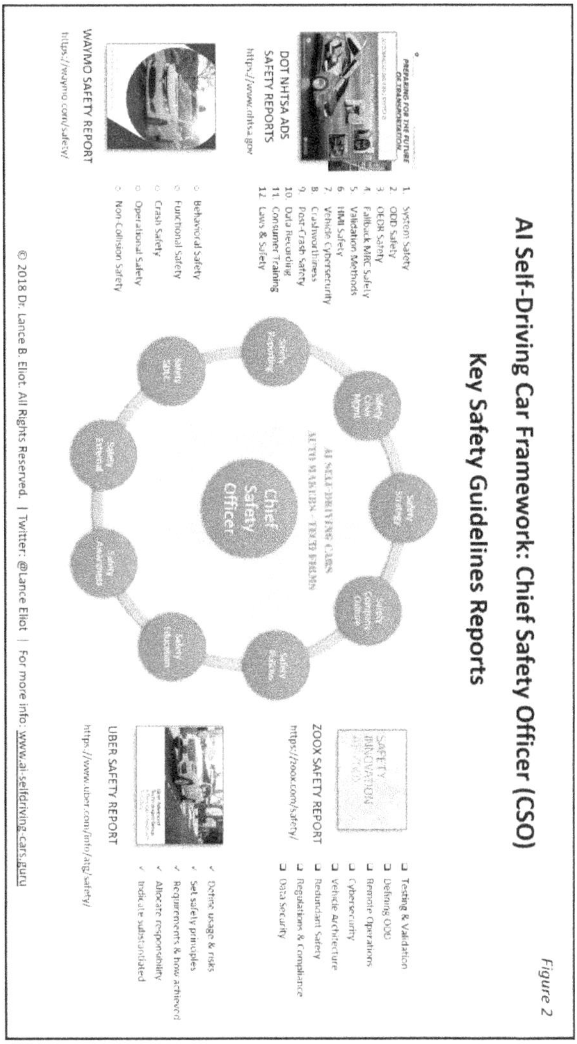
AI Self-Driving Car Framework: Chief Safety Officer (CSO)
Key Safety Guidelines Reports
Figure 2
DOT NHTSA ADS SAFETY REPORTS
https://www.nhtsa.gov
1. System Safety
2. ODD Safety
3. OEDR Safety
4. Fallback MRC Safety
5. Validation Methods
6. HMI Safety
7. Vehicle Cybersecurity
8. Crashworthiness
9. Post-Crash Safety
10. Data Recording
11. Consumer Training
12. Laws & Safety
WAYMO SAFETY REPORT
https://waymo.com/safety/
Behavioral Safety
Functional Safety
Crash Safety
Operational Safety
Non-Collision Safety
Chief Safety Officer
ZOOX SAFETY REPORT
https://zoox.com/safety/
Testing & Validation
Defining ODD
Remote Operations
Cybersecurity
Vehicle Architecture
Redundant Safety
Regulations & Compliance
Data Security
UBER SAFETY REPORT
https://www.uber.com/info/atg/safety/
Define usage & risks
Set safety principles
Requirements & how achieved
Allocate responsibility
Indicate substantiated
© 2018 Dr. Lance B. Eliot. All Rights Reserved. | Twitter: @Lance Eliot | For more info: www.ai-selfdriving-cars.guru

Returning to the safety topic, let's consider some additional facets.

Take a look at Figure 2.

I've listed some of the publicly available documents that are a useful cornerstone to getting up-to-speed about AI self-driving car safety.

The U.S. Department of Transportation (DOT) NHTSA has provided two reports that I especially find helpful about the foundations of safety related to AI self-driving cars. Besides providing background context, these documents also indicate the regulatory considerations that any auto maker or tech firm will need to be incorporating into their efforts. Both of these reports have been promulgated under the auspices of DOT Secretary Elaine Chao.

The version 2.0 report is here:
https://www.nhtsa.gov/sites/nhtsa.dot.gov/files/documents/13069a-ads2.0_090617_v9a_tag.pdf

The version 3.0 report is here:
https://www.transportation.gov/sites/dot.gov/files/docs/policy-initiatives/automated-vehicles/320711/preparing-future-transportation-automated-vehicle-30.pdf

I had earlier mentioned the Uber safety report, which is here: https://www.uber.com/info/atg/safety/

I also had mentioned the Zoox safety report, which is here: https://zoox.com/safety/

You would also likely find of us the Waymo safety report, which is here: https://waymo.com/safety/

I'd also like to give a shout out to Dr. Philip Koopman, a professor at CMU that has done extensive AI safety related research, which you can find at his CMU web site or at this company web site: https://edge-case-research.com/

As a former university professor, I too used to do research while at my university and also did so via an outside company. It's a great way to try and infuse the core foundational research that you typically do in a university setting with the more applied kind of efforts that you do while in industry.

I found it a handy combination. Philip and I seem to also end-up at many of the same AI self-driving car conferences and do so as speaker, panelists, or interested participants.

Conclusion

For those Chief Safety Officers of AI self-driving car firms that I've not mentioned herein, you are welcome to let me know that you'd like to be included in future updates that I do on this topic. Plus, if you have safety reports akin to the ones I've listed, I welcome taking a look at those reports and will be glad to mention those too.

One concern being expressed about the AI self-driving car industry is whether the matter of safety is being undertaken in a secretive manner that tends to keep each other of the auto makers or tech firms in the dark about what the other firms are doing. When you look at the car industry, clearly it is apparent that the auto makers have traditionally competed on their safety records and used that to their advantage in trying to advertise and sell their wares.

Critics have voiced that if the AI self-driving car industry perceives itself to also be competing with each other on safety, naturally there would be a basis to purposely avoid sharing about safety aspects with each other.

You can't seemingly have it both ways, in that if you are competing on safety then it is presumed to be a zero-sum game, those that do better on safety will sell more than those that do not, and why help a competitor to get ahead.

This mindset needs to be overcome. As mentioned earlier, it won't take much in terms of a few safety related bad outcomes to potentially stifle the entire AI self-driving car realm. If there is a public outcry, you can expect that this will push back at the auto makers and tech firms.

The odds are that regulators would opt to come into the industry with a much heavier hand. Funding for AI self-driving car efforts might dry up. The engine driving the AI self-driving car pursuits could grind to a halt.

There are efforts popping up to try and see if AI safety can become more widespread as an overt topic in the AI self-driving car industry.

It's tough though to overcome all of those NDA (Non-Disclosure Agreements) and concerns that proprietary matters might be disclosed. Regrettably, it might take a calamity to get enough heat to make things percolate more so, but I hope it doesn't come down to that.

The adoption of Chief Safety Officers into the myriad of auto makers and tech firms that are pursuing AI self-driving cars is a healthy sign that safety is rising in importance.

These positions have to be adopted seriously and with a realization at the firms that they cannot just put in place a role to somehow checkmark that they did so.

For Chief Safety Officers to do their job, they need to be at the top executive table and be considered part-and-parcel of the leadership team. I am also hoping that these Chief Safety Officers will bind together and become an across-the-industry "club" that can embrace a safety sharing mantra and use their positions and weight to get us further along on permeating safety throughout all aspects of AI self-driving cars. Let's make that into reality.

CHAPTER 3
BOUNDED VOLUMES AND AI SELF-DRIVING CARS

CHAPTER 3

BOUNDED VOLUMES AND AI SELF-DRIVING CARS

The car ahead of me on the freeway had several lengthy poles tied to the top of their midsized vehicle and the flopping poles were dangling far beyond the rear end of the zooming along car. In California, the legal requirement is that any overhanging or projecting items that are beyond four feet of the taillamps must be decorated with a red cloth or a fluorescent orange flag. And, if the matter is happening at night time, two red lights must also be attached to the projection too (per our California Vehicle Code CVC Section 35410).

None of those legal requirements were being met by the driver.

For the moment, it was daytime. In about an hour it would be dusk and then quickly nighttime. As a minimum, the red or orange flag should have been used, and I think it was a likely bet that the driver was going to be on the road past sunset too. Tsk, tsk, flouting the law.

In any case, the immediate concern was whether other drivers would realize that the poles were protruding.

Given the time of day and the dwindling sunshine and given that many here in Southern California drive maddingly and don't pay close attention to the road and roadway obstacles, I had little doubt that some nutty driver might accidentally get so close to the rear of the pole-totting car that those poles would potentially ram into a windshield.

Based on the nature of the poles and how they were tied down to the roof of the car, I gauged that the poles would be unlikely to poke a hole in the windshield of another car and probably not create much damage, other than a few scratches and dents, but the real problem would be the reaction of the driver that rammed into the poles.

Would the driver that hit the poles suddenly be shocked and surprised, and in that mental capacity opt to make a wild maneuver? Doing so at the pace of 65 miles per hour was bound to create havoc. All it takes is for one driver to do something untoward and it causes a cascading impact to other nearby drivers. Another consideration was whether those poles might be jostled by hitting a windshield and then spill onto the freeway, which could also create a cascading array of cars weaving and dodging those poles. More chances of cars hitting each other.

Did the driver of the car that had placed the poles onto their roof realize the problems inherent in their actions? Were they lazy in not putting on a red or orange flag, or did they assume it wasn't needed, or maybe they thought that it was too much trouble and assumed it was "obvious" that the poles were overhanging the car? Or, perhaps the driver figured that no other car would venture so close to their car that the protrusion would make a difference. If we always all kept the requisite distance from other cars based on the speed charts, such as one car length for every ten miles per hour (no one in Los Angeles seems to abide by this!), presumably you would not encounter those precariously dangling poles.

I kept my distance from the car.

Doing so though merely led to other cars deciding to jump in between me and the car ahead of me. The rule-of-thumb on our freeways is a dog-eat-dog world in which any available gaps are immediately considered available for intrusion. Indeed, some drivers here insist they are doing all the rest of us a great service by compacting traffic. In their minds, any unused gap between cars is unsightly wasted space and merely elongates the traffic woes on the freeway.

As other cars came into my lane, some appeared to notice the poles, while others did not. I saw one car that started into my lane, realized the poles were poking out, and the driver then retreated back into their own lane. Another car, one that was relatively close to the ground, a smaller sports car, smoothly went under the poles, doing so as the lane switching driver used my lane to get over into the next lane to my right. A typical move by a sports car driver. Why switch lanes one at a time when you can make a multi-lane swift switch-a-roo, the NASCAR way.

Eventually, the driver of the flaunting poles decided they were nearing their exit and began to move over toward the exit lane. When the driver made each lane switch, they seemed to misjudge the amount of distance they needed to safely have available. I doubt the driver was calculating the added length of the car by including the additional length of the overhanging poles. This driver not only didn't flag the poles, they seemed to not care about how the poles changed the dynamics of the driving task.

Sad, but not too surprising.

Most of us likely don't think too much about the overall size of our cars, at least not consciously per se. Once you get used to the size or dimensions of your car, you pretty much know it by heart. If you drive the same car over and over, each day, you can almost feel the outer edges of the car. You instinctively know if you can make the tight corner or squeeze your car into that parking space that you had your eye on.

In contrast, when you rent a car, assuming it is a different make and model from your usual car, it probably takes you a few minutes of driving to get used to the dimensions of the car.

I remember renting a large-sized SUV for a camping trip and it was hard at first to sense where the four corners of the car were. I parked in front of my house and suddenly realized that the SUV stuck out beyond the usual spot that I park my normal car. When I went over to the mall to get some groceries, a parking spot opened up near the store, but as I slowly maneuvered the car into the spot, I realized that trying to park the beast in a compact-sized space was not a good idea.

A quick question for you. Take a moment to visualize in your mind the car that you usually drive. What is the length of the car? What is the width of the car? Most people aren't readily able to state in feet or inches what the length and width is. They just "know" about how big their car is. They can feel it when they drive. The moment you try to parallel park your car, you often become acutely aware of the size, since you are trying to shove it into a spot that often times just barely allows it to fit.

What about the height of your car? Most people aren't so sure what their precise height of the car is. They can guess. They also generally are able to discern whether their car will be able to go underneath a roadway sign or a bridge. This can be tested though when you go through a drive-thru eatery and they have a posted sign that warns what the height limit is. I've seen some drivers that inched forward, unsure of whether their roof might hit something, especially if they had a ski rack or a surfboard rack on their rooftop.

In terms of estimating the size of something, I am reminded of a notable aspect that happened when my children were quite young. We had gone to a ceramics shop that allowed us to buy various ceramic objects and then paint them while there in the store. It was a fun activity. After painting the objects, you left them at the shop for a day or so, allowing the shop to cure them, and then we'd come to pick-up our now shiny painted ceramic objects.

Upon arriving at the store a few days after painting the objects, consisting of a ceramic bunny and ceramic egg (done for Easter!), we looked at them with tremendous glee and pride. They looked superb, like a professional had painted them. I asked the kids to go get two cardboard boxes from the other side of the store so we could put each of the ceramic objects into a box and safely transport them.

One of the kids came back with a box that was so small that neither the bunny and nor the egg could fit. The other one came back with a box that was quite large and would inadvertently allow the bunny or egg to likely roll around and possibly get damaged while carrying the box. I pointed out these discrepancies and politely requested that they try to find a box that might be a more appropriate fit. You might say a Goldilocks sized box, one that was not too small, and nor too large.

They happily did so. We then packed the bunny and the egg into each of their own respective boxes. A successful effort and one that to this day is showcased on my mantle, notably bringing those objects out into the open when Easter comes around, symbols of the love and joy that went into crafting them.

What does a ceramic Easter egg and bunny have to do with a car on the freeway with overhanging poles? Good question, and here's the answer. Judging the dimensions of a box needed to fully contain an Easter egg or bunny is akin to envisioning a kind of virtual box that might surround the dimensions of your car.

I'd like you to once again think about the car that you usually drive. This time, rather than trying to state the dimensions, instead try to imagine a box into which your car might fit. When I say the word box, I suppose you can think of it more like a container, like say a shipping container. If we were going to try and ship your car to someplace, what sized container (or box) would you need?

You could make a wild guess and select a container or box that is twice the size of your car. In that case, you'd be sure that the car would fit. But, suppose I told you that there was an added cost as the size of the container or box increases. Thus, aiming high is going to be more costly.

I'm sure you would then adjust your guess and aim at a smaller container or box. Suppose the container or box is too small? That won't do, since you need to make sure that every inch of your car fits into the container or box. You can't have anything stretching beyond the container or box. Ideally, you want the container or box to just fit, ensuring that all aspects of the car are contained within the box, and not being much larger since the added cost of the larger size is something you are trying to avoid.

From your school days, I'm sure that you know that this box or container is going to have three dimensions. If all three of the dimensions are the same, you have a cube. In which case, the volume of the cube is each side times each other, or the side cubed, often written as V = a^3. If the sides are unequal, the volume of the resultant cuboid is typically written as V = l x h x w. This consists of the length, times the height, and times the width. Some prefer to say that the width is the depth, which is fine if that's what you feel more comfortable with.

Most cars are pretty much in the shape of a cuboid, meaning that the length, height, and width differ. We don't need necessarily though to make the container or box in the shape of a cuboid. Maybe we could fit your car into a pyramid shape, the volume being 1/3 B x h. Or maybe into the shape of a sphere, the volume being 4/3 pi r^3. And so on.

The easiest way to imagine the container would be to assume it is going to be a cuboid shape. Admittedly, this might not be a very efficient container depending upon the shape of your car. If we used some other shape, either a regular one like a sphere or pyramid, maybe it would be a better fit. Or, if we could create the entire design of the container on our own, we might shape it in an irregular fashion, curving it here and there to make it fit in a skintight way with your car.

When trying to place your car into a container of some kind, let's refer to this as the Bounded Volume (BV). I want to have you help me put your car into a container, which will consist of some amount of volume, and will be bounded by the shape that we use.

The BV could be a regular shape and a relatively simplistic cube or cuboid. Or, you might conceive of another less usual shape, such as a cone or pyramid, or you might fashion a rather irregular shape that conforms in some other tighter manner to your car.

What does this have to do with AI self-driving cars?

At the Cybernetic AI Self-Driving Car Institute, we are developing AI software for self-driving cars. One of the intriguing aspects about AI self-driving cars, and an aspect often not much discussed, involves the need for the AI to be able to detect objects and essentially craft a Bounded Volume (a virtual container) around those detected objects. This is a key effort to the rest of the AI driving system and especially the virtual world modelling aspects.

Allow me to elaborate.

I'd like to first clarify and introduce the notion that there are varying levels of AI self-driving cars. The topmost level is considered Level 5. A Level 5 self-driving car is one that is being driven by the AI and there is no human driver involved. For the design of Level 5 self-driving cars, the auto makers are even removing the gas pedal, brake pedal, and steering wheel, since those are contraptions used by human drivers. The Level 5 self-driving car is not being driven by a human and nor is there an expectation that a human driver will be present in the self-driving car. It's all on the shoulders of the AI to drive the car.

For self-driving cars less than a Level 5, there must be a human driver present in the car. The human driver is currently considered the responsible party for the acts of the car. The AI and the human driver are co-sharing the driving task. In spite of this co-sharing, the human is supposed to remain fully immersed into the driving task and be ready at all times to perform the driving task. I've repeatedly warned about the dangers of this co-sharing arrangement and predicted it will produce many untoward results.

Let's focus herein on the true Level 5 self-driving car. Much of the comments apply to the less than Level 5 self-driving cars too, but the fully autonomous AI self-driving car will receive the most attention in this discussion.

Here's the usual steps involved in the AI driving task:

- Sensor data collection and interpretation
- Sensor fusion
- Virtual world model updating
- AI action planning
- Car controls command issuance

Another key aspect of AI self-driving cars is that they will be driving on our roadways in the midst of human driven cars too. There are some pundits of AI self-driving cars that continually refer to a utopian world in which there are only AI self-driving cars on the public roads. Currently there are about 250+ million conventional cars in the United States alone, and those cars are not going to magically disappear or become true Level 5 AI self-driving cars overnight.

Indeed, the use of human driven cars will last for many years, likely many decades, and the advent of AI self-driving cars will occur while there are still human driven cars on the roads. This is a crucial point since this means that the AI of self-driving cars needs to be able to contend with not just other AI self-driving cars, but also contend with human driven cars.

It is easy to envision a simplistic and rather unrealistic world in which all AI self-driving cars are politely interacting with each other and being civil about roadway interactions. That's not what is going to be happening for the foreseeable future. AI self-driving cars and human driven cars will need to be able to cope with each other.

Returning to the topic of the Bounded Volume, let's consider why this is such an important matter to the AI self-driving car.

The AI system of the self-driving car is going to have various sensory devices, including cameras, radar, ultrasonic, LIDAR, and so on. We'll focus on the cameras for the moment.

While the AI self-driving car is driving around, the cameras are capturing visual images of what is surrounding the self-driving car. These images are streaming into the cameras. On-board the self-driving car, there are computer processors that are tasked with analyzing those images. The image processing is looking to see if there are any street signs, and whether there are any nearby pedestrians, and whether there are cars nearby, etc. This has to happen in real-time. Time is crucial.

The image processing doesn't have the luxury of acting in a lackadaisical manner. When a car is moving along on the freeway at 65 miles per hour, and other cars are whizzing past at the same or faster speeds, there is not much time to spare when ascertaining the traffic situation. It is incumbent upon the image processing to as quickly as possible parse the images and identify what is happening.

A human driver takes for granted that they can see their surroundings. They usually don't put much thought into this aspect since it seems obvious and expected. Of course I can see that pedestrian across the street. Of course I can see that roadway speed limit sign. But, if I add heavy fog into the situation, the human driver will be reminded of how difficult it can be to sometimes see your surroundings. There is a lot more going on in your head than you might otherwise assume.

How does the image processing try to do the same thing that humans seem to do with ease (most of the time)?

Upon inspecting the streaming images, the image processors attempt to dissect the images and figure out what identifiable objects exist in the scene. Is there a pedestrian over there? Is that a bike rider? Is that a car up ahead? Is that a car to the right?

By-and-large, most of what you might see on the roadway is relatively predictable, meaning that you can expect to see human pedestrians, you can expect to possibly see animals such as dogs or deer, you can expect to see other cars, and so on. As a human, you've learned or somehow come to know that a pedestrian is a human that is walking, standing, sitting, or otherwise a human-like figure that likely has arms, legs, a head, a body, feet, hands, and other such elements.

While driving your car, you look across the street and see a figure that consists of a head, a body, arms, feet, and the rest. In your mind, you somehow click to the notion that it is a human. Oh, but wait, it turns out that it is a statue of a famous president, placed at the corner of that upcoming street. It looked at first glance like a human, a living breathing human, but it turns out to be a statue of a human. Obviously, that's quite different.

Why is it different? The odds are that you aren't expecting the statue to suddenly move along and try to cross the street. If it was a human standing there, you'd be watching to see what the human is doing. Are they looking as though they want to cross the street? Is the human merely standing or starting to walk or run? How far from the street is the human? If the human runs versus walks, how soon might they appear in the street?

Because of the somewhat predictability of objects that we might see while driving, it is possible to use Machine Learning or Deep Learning to try and prepare the image processing to be able to detect objects that are being seen by the camera. We can feed hundreds, maybe thousands upon thousands of images of pedestrians into a deep or large-scale multi-layer artificial neural network, and try to get it to pattern match on those images. You want the pattern matching to be general enough to detect a wide set of variations, rather than becoming fixed on particular shapes or sizes.

Once the image processing has been trained, we'd put it into the on-board AI system of the self-driving car and have presumably tuned the image processing so that it can work quickly. Recall that I earlier emphasized the importance of time and the speed of processing. Having a great image processing system based on Deep Learning won't do much good if it takes say 5 seconds to identify a potentially life-threatening object and for which during those 5 seconds the self-driving car has proceeded ahead unabated and rams into the object.

The images streaming into the cameras of the self-driving car are likely to contain many objects. Think about the times you've driven in a downtown area at rush hour, such as in New York City or downtown Los Angeles. You might have many dozens of pedestrians. There might be animals such as people walking their dogs. There are cars to your left, cars to your right, cars behind you, cars ahead of you. A delivery person might be pushing a cart that contains delivery packages.

It is chaos!

Not only do you need to discern those objects, you also need to identify where the buildings are, where the curbs of the street are, and so on. There might be trees along the side of the street. There could be fire hydrants. A slew of objects is in that scene. If you've ever been with a novice teenage driver as they for the first-time drive in a busy downtown area, you can nearly see their eyes pop out of their head and their head explode as they try to notice and keep track of the myriad of objects.

The AI system on-board the self-driving car has to do the same.

One means to try and cope with the complexity of the scene involves classifying objects. The image processing tries to determine that the object standing at the street corner is a human, a pedestrian, and classifies the object as such. This gets posted into an overall model of what the surroundings consist of. The model, a virtual model of the real-world, provides a kind of mapping of what objects there are, along with what they are, and what they might do.

Based on the virtual world model, the AI action planning portion of the on-board system will assess the situation and try to determine what actions to have the self-driving car undertake. If the virtual world model indicates that a car is directly ahead of the self-driving car, and the brake lights are on, and the car ahead is braking and the AI self-driving car is coming rapidly upon the stopping car, the AI action planner has to ascertain what to do.

The AI action planner examines the virtual world model and tries to determine what action makes the best sense to initiate. Maybe the self-driving car can swerve around the car that's stopping. This requires examining the virtual world model to see what is to the right and left of the car ahead. Are there pedestrians standing there? Is there a car in the way? These and a variety of what-if scenarios need to be rapidly explored.

Time is again crucial. If the AI action planner looks at twenty different what-if scenarios, it could use up so much time that the opportunity to swerve is now gone anyway. Keep in mind that the AI action planner needs to emit commands to the self-driving car controls, and those controls need to receive the commands and then undertake the physical actions indicated, such as giving gas to the accelerator or turning the steering wheel. That takes time. Suppose it takes 3 seconds to get the swerve underway, but it has taken meanwhile 2 seconds to decide upon the swerving action, it might be too late to further consider the swerving as viable.

Imagine that a bike rider is also involved in the scenario of having to decide what to do about a car that ahead is unexpectedly coming to a stop. Maybe one option for the AI is to swerve the self-driving car into the bike lane and squeeze between the car that is stopping and a bike rider that is in the bike lane. Is there enough room there to fit into that tight space?

This brings us back to the earlier discussion about Bounded Volumes.

The image processing is usually established to not only try and find objects in the scene, but also classify those objects and appoint a Bounded Volume or virtual container to the object. The car ahead that is stopping will have been assigned a Bounded Volume associated with that car, depending upon the dimensions and size of the car. Likewise, the bike and the bike rider, which we'll say are one object consisting of two things, we'll assign a Bounded Volume or virtual container that encompasses that bike rider and bike.

Why assign these make-believe containers to the objects? Well, as mentioned, suppose the AI is having to try and decide whether to slip between the stopping car that's ahead and the bike rider that's in the bike lane. The self-driving car itself has its own Bounded Volume, which it should already be familiar with, and it needs to try and calculate whether the Bounded Volume of the self-driving car and fit between the Bounded Volume of the car ahead and the Bounded Volume of the bike rider.

To visualize this, consider cubes or cuboids for each of these objects. We have a cuboid representing the self-driving car. We have a cuboid representing the car ahead. We have a cuboid representing the bike rider. Via the camera, let's assume we can gauge the distance that's between the right side of the car ahead and the left edge of the bike rider. The width of the self-driving car has to be able to fit into that distance, if there's any chance of sliding to the right of the stopping car.

In the virtual world model, we'd have represented the Bounded Volumes of the car ahead, the bike rider, and the self-driving car. Based on the virtual world model aspects, the AI tries to ascertain whether the self-driving car can fit into the gap between the car ahead Bounded Volume and the Bounded Volume of the bike rider, as based on the Bounded Volume of the self-driving car.

Though you might think this is an easy geometry problem and involves easy mathematics, I'd like to point out that there's a lot more to this decision making.

The car ahead is a Bounded Volume moving at a particular rate of speed and going in a particular direction. Same is said for the self-driving car. Same is said for the bike rider. They are all in-motion. This means that making predictions will involve uncertainty about what will happen next.

Suppose the bike rider opts to suddenly swerve to their left, shortening the gap between them and the car ahead. Suppose the car ahead opts to swerve toward the bike rider, shortening the gap. The world is not stationary. The virtual world has to account for the motion of objects. This motion is not guaranteed to continue in any straightforward manner. The objects can likely alter their path, even if it maybe doesn't make logical sense for them to do so.

In this case, it might not seem logical that the bike rider would want to swerve toward the car that's ahead. Dumb move! We don't know that this really is a dumb move, since there might be something else happening related to the bike rider. Suppose a pedestrian holding a dog on a leash has accidently let the dog go, and the dog is rushing onto the street. The bike rider, seeing the rushing dog, decides to try and swerve to the left of the dog, not perhaps realizing that the car adjacent to them is stopping and might opt to swerve into the bike lane.

In the virtual world model, did the AI system have the pedestrian modeled and the dog modeled? Maybe the image processing could not detect those objects, perhaps the pedestrian and dog were obscured by some other objects like a light pole. In that case, the AI action planner is "blind" to the notion that a pedestrian is standing there with a dog and that the dog has gotten loose.

Notice that this brings up numerous facets about the Bounded Volumes and the virtual world model.

If there is not a representation in the virtual model of real-world objects because those real-world objects were not detected by the image processing, it means that the AI system is having to cope with a virtual world that is not an accurate depiction of the real-world. The AI action planner can end-up making life-or-death driving decisions based on this omitted information, perhaps leading to a calamity.

Suppose the image processing wasn't sure what the clump was near the corner and it consisted of the human walking the dog, which could be detected on the other side of a light pole, and the image processing could discern that something was there, a kind of unidentifiable blob. The image processing might not be able to classify it, but at least it could tag in the virtual world model that there's an object there, along with imputing a Bounded Volume that encapsulates the blob.

Once the dog gets loose, this would hopefully be detected by the cameras, and the image processing might now be able to discern that there is a pedestrian there and a dog there, two separate objects, and had been the overall blob that had earlier been posted at that location. The virtual world model would then be updated accordingly.

Why does it matter that the dog is now a Bounded Volume of its own? A dog as a classification means that you can predict various aspects of its behavior. A dog can move in certain ways at certain speeds. A human can move in certain ways at certain speeds. The classification of an object helps to anticipate what the object might do. It aids the AI action planner in deciding upon the action to be taken.

Let's pretend for a moment that the dog is instead a skateboard that the pedestrian has let loose and is rolling into the street. I say this because of what I am about to suggest. If the AI action planner has to calculate what might need to be hit in order to save the life of the bike rider, I think we'd all agree that hitting the skateboard would be preferable. This highlights the kind of ethical choices that the AI system needs to make, doing so in real-time.

The Bounded Volume that you craft to represent an object needs to be large enough to accommodate the overall object and yet not so large that it unnecessarily inflates the size of the actual object. In the case of trying to squeeze between the bike rider and the car ahead of the self-driving car, if the BV for the bike rider is overly large it might deny the possibility of fitting between the bike rider and the car ahead, even though in reality it might have been feasible.

On the other hand, if the BV is overly skintight, it is possible that a miscalculation could occur of striking the real-world object by having gotten too close to it. This goes back to the earlier point about arriving at a Goldilocks size for the BV in terms of representing the real-world object.

One of the most essential aspects of the virtual world model involves discerning whether there is going to be an intersecting of two or more Bounded Volumes. For example, if the Bounded Volume or virtual container representing the self-driving car is going to intersect with the Bounded Volume or virtual container of the bike rider, this needs to be anticipated and dealt with by the AI action planner.

If two or more Bounded Volumes are anticipated to intersect, the possibility of a collision arises. I'll use the word collision to refer to a circumstance of two objects that actually brush against each other or ram into each other, physically doing so. When I use the word intersecting, it means that there is the potential for an actual collision, though it is not necessarily a collision per se. This depends upon the amount of inflated size that we have for the Bounded Volumes involved.

Suppose the bike rider is represented by a BV that is twice the actual size of the bike rider. This implies a kind of virtual buffer or cushion, allowing for wiggle room of the real-world object within the imaginary container that we've concocted.

A self-driving car entering into the Bounded Volume of the bike rider might not actually hit the bike rider, since there's that extra space within the virtual container. In a sense, the inflated size of the BV can provide a margin of error into which another BV can wander and yet not actually touch the real-world object therein.

I'm sure that you likely think about your own car in the same way. You are apt to have a sense that there is an outer boundary of a few inches beyond the actual size of your car. When you try to park your car into a rather confining parking spot, you are subliminally aware that you have a little bit of a cushion of space. As you get closer and closer to another parked car, you begin to sweat about whether you are undermining that cushion and getting so close that you'll rub against or scratch the other car.

This also brings up the earlier topic about overhanging or protruding aspects of your car.

If you have an antenna on your car that goes upward a few feet, above the roof height of your car, you often tend to ignore the antenna as being part of a kind of Bounded Volume, under the belief that if the antenna hits something it will just do so lightly and spring back. On the other hand, your side mirrors typically have to be included in your sense of a Bounded Volume due to their possibility of breaking off or damaging another car if you rub against the side mirrors while parking your car (many cars today have rejiggered the side mirrors to pivot inward when touched, allowing some flexibility in their positioning).

Remember too my story of the car that had poles dangling from the rooftop of the car. What do you think the Bounded Volume of that car should be? You could make the Bounded Volume consist of the car only and not include the added aspect of the dangling poles, but this means that the AI self-driving car might not calculate the possibilities of hitting those dangling poles. If you make the Bounded Volume to include the dangling poles, the overall size of the BV is larger and might preclude the AI from realizing that it might be able to fit underneath those poles, which recall that the sports car in my story was able to do so.

Along those lines, the other aspect is whether the Bounded Volume is a regular shape such as a cube or cuboid, or whether you want to have it be an irregular shape. By using an irregular shape, you could potentially encompass the car that has the dangling poles and then also encompass the dangling poles, but not have one overarching cube or cuboid that tries to do so. The shape would be tailored to the contours of the actual object.

The problem of having an irregular shaped contour will be the added mathematical and computational effort involved in dealing with the BV in the virtual world model. Time is crucial and making the BV into an irregular shape is going to cost you in terms of added computer processing time. There is a tradeoff involved between using the simpler shapes which are computationally less expensive versus using a complex shape that chews-up computational processing time.

There are various algorithmic tricks that you need to employ when trying to make the virtual world model as fast as possible. For example, when trying to determine whether two or more Bounded Volumes are going to intersect, you can use the Separating Axis Theorem (SAT), a quick method to determine the minimum penetration vector involving two BV's. Essentially, you mathematically try to see if there is a line or plane that can fit between two Bounded Volumes, and if so, the two are not yet intersecting.

One aspect that I often get asked about at conferences involves whether the virtual world model and its use of Bounded Volumes as virtual containers representing real-world objects can be calculated outside of the self-driving car such as in the cloud of the auto maker or tech firm. You would normally expect that all of these calculations have to take place in the on-board AI system of the self-driving car, since the timing aspects are so vital. That's why AI self-driving cars are chockfull of the fastest processors and tend to require a large amount of computer memory on-board.

The key problem with trying to place the virtual world model into the cloud would be the latency involved in conveying the matter to and from the cloud by the AI self-driving car.

The amount of time involved in shoving up to the cloud the data from the AI self-driving car that came from the sensors, and the amount of time to get a result transmitted back down to the self-driving car, chews up so much time that you might not be able to have the AI self-driving car acting in a timely manner.

Usually, any kind of OTA (Over-The-Air) aspects of the AI self-driving car is going to be done for matters that are not time crucial per se. At the end of a day of driving, for example, the AI self-driving car might push up to the cloud the days' worth of collected data, and meanwhile the cloud might be pushing down into the AI self-driving car the latest patches and updates.

There are hopes that with the advent of 5G, along with edge computing, perhaps these aspects can take place in a more real-time way, though it is still seemingly unlikely to happen fast enough to be in-the-loop during actual driving activities.

Some have proposed a hybrid approach of having a virtual world model within the on-board system and a mirrored version in the cloud. The cloud-based version would be used to explore "longer term" timeframe actions of the AI self-driving car, such as examining what's taking place some distance ahead of the self-driving car. Meanwhile, the on-board AI system is focusing on the more immediate tactical aspects.

This splitting of the effort allows the exploiting of say exascale supercomputing power at the cloud level and can provided an added boost to what the on-board AI is able to undertake.

Another aspect about the virtual world model involves the use of Machine Learning or Deep Learning.

Much of the virtual world model efforts are primarily logic-based and involve coding up the calculations and predictions that come from the virtual world model.

Interestingly, trying to discern patterns of driving behaviors is possible by leveraging the virtual world model. By collecting data about the virtual world model over time, you can use Deep Learning to identify traffic and driver behaviors, which can then be used for improving the predictive capabilities of the AI system.

Conclusion

There used to be an advertising campaign about how plumbers were the unseen and unheralded heroes of making sure that your house pipes and water were flowing right. Most people don't put much thought toward their plumbing, other than when it breaks, and water is spilling onto their floors. You just assume that the plumbing is done right and until or if it goes on the fritz, you aren't concerned about it.

The virtual world model and the Bounded Volumes in AI self-driving cars are similar to the plumbing and the plumbers. You don't see much attention provided to these elements.

Instead, all the glory seems to go toward the sensors. There are weekly news updates about how a new LIDAR sensor is better than another one, or how a camera for AI self-driving cars has come out that has better vision capabilities than present ones. Sensors, sensor, sensors.

As hopefully is now evident, if you have a lousy virtual world model, or at least one that is not timely and well-tuned, it won't matter how good the sensors are, since it's going to be a mess of knowing what surrounds the self-driving car, and the AI action planner will be blind or thrown a kilter by a lack of having a proper and timely indication of the surroundings.

Likewise, if the Bounded Volumes are poorly representing the real-world objects, the AI action planner won't be able to discern what makes sense in terms of avoiding objects and also anticipating the intersecting of objects.

For those AI developers that toil away in dealing with this kind of plumbing, let's herald them for their efforts. Though perhaps unseen and not appreciated, there is an impressive amount of complexity and incredible effort involved in these matters, plus much room left to advance these capabilities, which ultimately will make-or-break the advent of safe and successful AI self-driving cars.

CHAPTER 4

MICRO-MOVEMENT BEHAVIORS AND AI SELF-DRIVING CARS

CHAPTER 4
MICRO-MOVEMENT BEHAVIORS AND AI SELF-DRIVING CARS

I was eagerly awaiting making a right turn on a red light at a busy intersection that led onto the always hectic Pacific Coast Highway (PCH).

Dutifully stopping behind the crosswalk line, I could not quite see the prevailing traffic that was coming over a hilly portion of PCH that fed down through this particular area. The layout meant that you could not be fully sure whether the lanes were free to drive into and at any moment a raging car might seemingly leap over the hill and barrel into you if you prematurely had opted to make the treacherous right turn.

Being in a hurry, I decided that I would just go for it and gunned my engine to swiftly propel my car through the right turn and into the lane of traffic that seemed to be empty and available. Unfortunately, in the split second that I had hit the gas, sure enough a car appeared suddenly at the crest of the hill and I could see that it was intent on using the lane that I was about to occupy. Some driver's in my shoes might proceed anyway and force the other driver to either hit their own brakes or swerve to another lane to avoid me, the lane intruder.

I didn't want to chance the possibility of having the nearing car rear-end my car, plus I would obviously have been in the wrong for my actions. I urgently moved my foot from the accelerator over to the brake and jammed down hard, forcing my car to come to a heart stopping halt. Yes, I was protruding somewhat into the lane, but it was not enough to cause the other car to undertake a diversion or hit their own brakes. They could sweep past my now half-in half-out car and proceed without skipping a beat.

The story might end there, and I suppose might have been unworthy perhaps of telling if that's all that happened, except for one little and quite important fact. There was a car that was behind me, also waiting at the red light, and the driver had been apparently hopeful of making the right turn as I did so. This car had inched its way up to my rear bumper and was earnestly urging me to make the right turn swiftly. I'm sure you've had this kind of eager beaver behind you. They breath down your neck and get irritated and upset if you don't make a highly expedient right turn on red.

Well, this other driver had assumed that since I was gunning my engine and leaping forward, they might as well do the same. I guess we were going to be like two sprinters that heard the starting gun go off and it was then a race to get underway. When I opted to hit my brakes, doing so suddenly, the driver behind me was caught by surprise.

Allow me a moment to carp about that driver. In my view, if they are going to follow behind me with nary any space allotted between the two of us, it is incumbent upon that driver to be fully ready to react in whatever way the driver ahead of them acts. It is a solemn golden rule of follow-the-leader in car driving. Anyone that is going to play the follow-the-leader game and do so without a safety cushion, they need to mirror the actions of the leader and do so with the same quickness of any efforts by the leader. Anyone that can't do that should not be participating in follow-the-leader. Just wanted to get that off my chest.

In any case, the car behind me almost rammed into my car. Thankfully, it was almost and not an actual hit. The driver swerved to avoid hitting the back of my car and jammed against the curb where the right turn was. I could see in my rearview mirror that the driver was upset – at me, and was apparently cursing and making unmentionable finger movements expressing their displeasure at my actions.

I usually try to calculate the moves of any cars behind me in whatever driving actions I take, and likely normally would have realized the other driver was within an inch of my car and not therefore have rocketed forward, but in this case I was in a hurry and assumed the other driver would be savvy enough to realize the potential for a rapid braking due to the PCH hilly road shape. Too bad for them that they miscalculated. It didn't look like there was any actual damage to their car and so I proceed to now continue the right turn and make my way to my looming appointment.

I did have in the back of mind a concern that this driver might get themselves worked up into a road rage. You know how that can happen in these kinds of circumstances. The driver was mad at me. They were in a hurry. I fully expected the driver to now also make the right turn, and then attempt to catch-up with me, coming alongside of my car to make more reprehensible gestures at me. Or, perhaps even try to run me off the road. You never know what crazy things people might do.

When you think about the situation, I probably accelerated for just a fraction of a second or so. My car appeared to leap forward like a leopard. The total distance covered was just a handful of feet. Luckily my brakes were darned good and when I jammed my foot onto the brake pedal the car came to an amazingly crisp stop. You could almost say that the whole thing happened in the blink of an eye.

I'm not sure that any of the other nearby drivers noticed what happened. The car that was barreling down PCH that I had wanted to avoid hitting was probably just happy that my car was not in their way.

Other cars at the intersection that were waiting to go were probably looking at the red light and expecting it to soon turn green. All in all, I'd bet that only me and the car behind me were aware of the dance that the two of us undertook.

I've told you this story to bring up something that is quite important and yet often overlooked as an aspect of human driving behavior, namely the use of micro-movements when driving.

A micro-movement is considered a somewhat subtle driving action that exists somewhere in the gray area between doing an overt and obvious driving maneuver and doing essentially no noticeable driving maneuvering at all.

Some human drivers are oblivious to the nature of micro-movements. These drivers are blind to noticing micro-movements and can't readily tell you what a micro-movement looks like. Their attention to the driving task is based on wholescale movements and maneuvers, ones that are stand out like a brass band and are so obvious that you'd truly need to be blind to miss them. Anything less than the outright maneuver of a car is totally lost on them.

I remember one colleague at work that used to drive several of us out to lunch on Friday's. He drove his car like it was a Sherman tank. He was master of the roadway, and no one dared to get in his way. This vividly became evident on one occasion involving him and a car that appeared to be driven by someone lost and unfamiliar with the local streets.

The driver ahead of us was driving relatively slowly in terms of being just a tad below the posted speed limit. The car had several times started toward the curb as though the driver was thinking of stopping or parking, and yet the driver continued ahead. It seemed apparent to me and everyone else in the car that my colleague was driving that this other driver was trying to figure out where they were and wanted to maybe park at a specific address.

My clueless colleague did not notice the antics of the other car. Driving his car like a take-no-prisoners tank commander, he nearly rolled over the other car when it tried to make a few of those potential darts to the curb. If it had been me doing our lunch journey driving, I would have given the other car some added space to allow them to do these swaying kinds of motions. Plus, I would have swung into the left lane and gone around the other car, hoping to then avoid the situation entirely of dealing with the other car.

After we made it to the lunch, I asked my colleague if he had noticed the car that had been in front of us. What do you mean, he asked, what was to be noticed? When I told him about the micro-movements of the other driver, my colleague insisted that I was making it up. It was a gag, he insisted. Fortunately, my fellow lunch time eaters all chimed in about that car. They had all noticed it too. Of course, this only inspired my colleague to claim that it was a conspiracy and we were all ganging up on him.

You don't necessarily need to be in a car to see the micro-movements of other cars. I ride my bike quite a bit and anyone that is hopeful of surviving the riding of a bike in city traffic is likely to be an expert on the micro-movement evidenced by cars and those wacky human drivers.

Just last week, I was in the bike lane, minding my own business, and I had a car that zoomed along and passed me, doing so with a flourish. The car traffic up ahead was stopping to deal with a roadway construction effort, and I lamented in my mind that this "jerk" was going too fast toward it. In my book, the driver ought to be slowing down and getting ready to figure out how to safety navigate around the street repair efforts.

Due to the bunching up of the car traffic, I caught up with the traffic since the bike lane was unimpeded. It was one of those rare cases whereby you can go faster along than the cars can. The cars were jockeying for position to find a means to navigate around the street crew and meanwhile I was rocketing ahead on my bike. Though I relish a moment of going faster than cars, I also know that doing so is tantamount to poking at a slumbering beast that can awaken at any moment and attack you.

Remember the car that had zoomed past me? It became the slumbering beast. The driver was anxious about being snagged in the snarled traffic. I could see that the car was nudging somewhat into the bike lane. At first, it was merely a slight intrusion. I had a hunch that the driver was testing the waters about whether or not he could come directly into the bike lane, doing so to use it as a means to escape the stunted traffic and get ahead of the other "sheep" that were stuck in the pile of cars.

I moved to the rightmost position of the bike lane and was kissing the curb. This was a defensive preparatory move by me. I also had my hands squarely on the brake handles of my bike, ready to use my brakes if needed. I observed the tires of the car that was inching into the bike lane and could see that the driver was becoming more decisive about angling toward the bike lane.

Sure enough, he then maneuvered completely into the bike lane, which was not only dangerous for me, but there were other bike riders in it too. The madcap driver completely upended all of the bike riders, not by the car actually hitting the riders, and instead by the bike riders all swerving this way or that way to avoid the intruding car, like bowling pins at a bowling alley. Have you ever seen those televised bike races in France and seen those moments when the bike riders appear to fall and collide all at once, it was about the same here. Sacre Bleu!

Sometimes a micro-movement can be signaled by something other than the car itself.

For example, a human driver puts their arm out the driver's side window to wave you around them, or maybe they point at something up ahead to forewarn you that there's a big pothole in the road. Hand motions though can be confusing and at times not meant to be a car movement indication.

I watched the other day as one driver put his hand and arm fully out the window and seemed to be waving the appendage up and down, rather frantically, which I wasn't sure what this might portend. Maybe the earth had opened a giant sinkhole and the road ahead was merely a huge ditch? When I opted to drive around the car, figuring I'd need to be on my toes and contend with whatever I might encounter, I could hear loud music being played on the speakers in the car -- I surmised that the hand and arm motions were just his way of keeping a beat to the music.

A driver's head can be another form of a clue about driving behavior. I'm sure you had times when you've been driving and could see the head of the driver in the car ahead of you. The driver perhaps turns their head to the right, and you are able to predict that the driver is going to try and either swing into the lane to the right or start to make a right turn.

Another head signal involves a head nod, often used when at a four-way stop and the other driver wants to showcase that either you should go or they want to proceed.

Let's focus on the micro-movements of cars that are evidenced by the actual car and set aside for now the kinds of micro-movements that humans themselves might undertake with their own bodies.

Here are some the key ways that micro-movements can appear:

- Angling of the wheels of the car
- Leftward leaning of the car
- Rightward leaning of the car
- Stuttered motion of the car (start/stop)
- Car lurches (sudden motion)
- Riding of the brakes
- Etc.

These aforementioned car movement indications are considered micro-movements when they are done in a subtle manner. It's a kind of a tease. Just a little bit of showing of the leg, as it were.

Some might liken this to a "tell" in a sport like basketball. When playing basketball competitively, you might give a movement of your head that seems to say you are going to make a run to the basket, and the other player covering you can potentially read the tell and get positioned to block you. This can all happen in an instant. It can happen too before the player with the ball has actually moved their feet toward the basket and taken any other overt actions.

If you like to play poker, you certainly know about the tell or clues that other players often inadvertently show. When I was in college, I played a Saturday poker game with some of my buddies. One member of the tight knit group was well-known for trying to bluff his way on hands where he had nothing of use in his cards. It was the classic saying about the notion that weak means strong, and strong means weak, namely that whenever he tried to make it seem like he had all aces, it really meant he had junk. This was his tell.

Another player had a tell that involved pushing his glasses up his nose and toward his eyes.

We all eventually figured out that this was his tell. It meant that he was lying about whatever he might be saying. None of us revealed the tell to him, and we kept it each to ourselves, relishing it. After months of this, one of the pack opted to tell him about his tell.

At first, he was angry that we had noticed the tell. He was also angry that we had not revealed it to him, though he sheepishly realized that he probably would not have told any of us about our tells. It dawned on him that if we had become conditioned to his tell, he could use that conditioning to his advantage. For a few weeks, he would purposely push his glasses on his nose, doing so to make us think he was lying, even though he might be telling the truth. We got caught like a hungry fish on a shiny lure. He made some good money by exploiting his own tell.

One of the members of the group had been oblivious to the tell. When it was finally revealed to everyone at one of the poker games, this particular member was shocked. What tell? He had never noticed that our friend was often pushing his glasses up further on his nose.

This highlights my earlier point about micro-movements of cars. Some people notice them, some do not. And it also highlights another very important point. You cannot for sure bet on a micro-movement since there is no guarantee it will ultimately graduate into becoming a full-on movement. Not all tells blossom. You need to assess each one, along with the situation at-hand, and ascertain whether the micro-movement is telling you something of substance or not.

Let's also make clear what isn't a micro-movement. If someone completely cranks the wheels over to make a full turn, I don't think we can really consider that to be a micro-movement. Only if the driver had just slightly angled the wheels, perhaps doing so to get ready for a turn, or maybe they were almost subconsciously starting the turn, those are situations of a micro-movement.

One of the ways to study micro-movements often involves observing teenage novice drivers. There are some newbie drivers that stretch out every driving move they make. When they are told to make a turn at the corner up ahead, they start the turn a quarter mile beforehand. When they see a stop sign, even if its at a distance of a football field length away, the novice driver often starts to tap those brakes, getting the car slowed down, slowly, really slowly.

Those tend to be exaggerated micro-movements. Most seasoned drivers are apt to make much more subtle micro-movements. Those weathered drivers have become ingrained in how they drive a car. They aren't necessarily aware that they are using micro-movements.

Similar to my story about my poker playing friend that ended-up exploiting his tell, there are some savvy drivers that like to use their micro-movements in an exploitive way. These drivers often assume that other drivers will notice the micro-movement and then back-off or otherwise give way to the driver that is using the micro-movements.

This happens a lot in parking lots. When cars are driving around and around trying to find a parking spot, it can become a gamesmanship effort of who suggests they found an open spot first. You've likely seen two cars that came open an open spot, and the cars are facing each other head-to-head. Which one will get the spot? If one driver angles their wheels, it can be a kind of assertion that they have tagged the spot and are going to aggressively make their way into the spot.

This can at times create more problems than it solves.

Suppose you have two cars facing each other, trying to vie for a parking spot, and each makes a wheel angling micro-movement. Is this a tie game? Will one driver take Umbridge that the other driver appears to be claiming the spot?

We also need to consider the clueless driver that doesn't even notice the other car is angling its wheels.

Or, you can also have the driver that sees the micro-movement and opts to ignore it, acting as though they didn't notice it, so they can appear to be blissfully ignorant as they take the spot (and later claim they didn't realize the other car was trying to go for it). That's a sly move.

Besides teenage novice drivers showcasing micro-movements, there's another kind of driver that can do likewise, namely a drunk or DUI (Driving Under the Influence) driver. When someone is just partially drunk, they often exhibit numerous micro-movements. They do so because they are either unsure of what driving path they are going to take, or they are lacking in their mental facilities and are erratically coping with the car controls.

If you are a seasoned driver that watches for drunk drivers, I'm sure you've seen many such micro-movements. That being said, once a drunk or DUI driver has gotten fully engulfed by their mind-altering influence, their car directing movements are bound to become the opposite of micro-movements. The driver make overt and extremely overstated movements. Any subtlety about their driving is now completely gone.

What does this have to do with AI self-driving cars?

At the Cybernetic AI Self-Driving Car Institute, we are developing AI software for self-driving cars. One aspect that is not yet getting much attention involves the micro-movements of driver behavior, which some consider an edge or corner case problem.

Allow me to elaborate.

I'd like to first clarify and introduce the notion that there are varying levels of AI self-driving cars. The topmost level is considered Level 5. A Level 5 self-driving car is one that is being driven by the AI and there is no human driver involved. For the design of Level 5 self-driving cars, the auto makers are even removing the gas pedal, brake pedal, and steering wheel, since those are contraptions used by human drivers.

The Level 5 self-driving car is not being driven by a human and nor is there an expectation that a human driver will be present in the self-driving car. It's all on the shoulders of the AI to drive the car.

For self-driving cars less than a Level 5, there must be a human driver present in the car. The human driver is currently considered the responsible party for the acts of the car. The AI and the human driver are co-sharing the driving task. In spite of this co-sharing, the human is supposed to remain fully immersed into the driving task and be ready at all times to perform the driving task. I've repeatedly warned about the dangers of this co-sharing arrangement and predicted it will produce many untoward results.

Let's focus herein on the true Level 5 self-driving car. Much of the comments apply to the less than Level 5 self-driving cars too, but the fully autonomous AI self-driving car will receive the most attention in this discussion.

Here's the usual steps involved in the AI driving task:

- Sensor data collection and interpretation
- Sensor fusion
- Virtual world model updating
- AI action planning
- Car controls command issuance

Another key aspect of AI self-driving cars is that they will be driving on our roadways in the midst of human driven cars too. There are some pundits of AI self-driving cars that continually refer to a utopian world in which there are only AI self-driving cars on the public roads. Currently there are about 250+ million conventional cars in the United States alone, and those cars are not going to magically disappear or become true Level 5 AI self-driving cars overnight.

Indeed, the use of human driven cars will last for many years, likely many decades, and the advent of AI self-driving cars will occur while there are still human driven cars on the roads. This is a crucial point since this means that the AI of self-driving cars needs to be able to contend with not just other AI self-driving cars, but also contend with human driven cars.

It is easy to envision a simplistic and rather unrealistic world in which all AI self-driving cars are politely interacting with each other and being civil about roadway interactions. That's not what is going to be happening for the foreseeable future. AI self-driving cars and human driven cars will need to be able to cope with each other.

Returning to the topic of micro-movements of human driving behavior, let's consider how these actions come to play in the design and development of AI self-driving cars.

I usually get asked two questions about this topic, which comes up when I am speaking at industry conferences.

First, does it matter whether AI self-driving cars are developed such that they will be able to detect the micro-movements of other cars?

My short answer is that yes, it does matter and AI developers at the auto makers and tech firms should be including this capability into their AI self-driving cars.

Most of the auto makers and tech firms are not yet encompassing the detection of micro-movements. This lack of attention to the topic is due to several reasons.

Some of the auto makers and tech firms are oblivious to the nature of micro-movements and so it isn't even a matter that has reached their awareness to do something about. Of those that are aware of it, they are already so taxed with trying to do straightforward driving tasks that trying to add the assessment and use of micro-movements in determining how to drive the AI self-driving car is an overload for them right now.

Indeed, many of those AI developers would contend that analyzing micro-movements and using those analyses for guiding the driving behavior of the AI is an edge or corner case. In the parlance of the AI field, anything judged to be a corner case or edge case is something that can be put on the backburner. It is not at the core of what they believe needs to be done. As such, they might consider micro-movements interesting, but not vital enough to warrant being on the pressing To-Do list.

I'd like to challenge that assumption about the low-priority assigned to dealing with micro-movements. I would argue that being able to detect and decipher the micro-movements of other drivers is a core driving skill. It allows you to anticipate what other cars and their drivers are potentially going to do. By knowing about micro-movements, seasoned human drivers can keep themselves out of potential troubles, which otherwise those human drivers that seem out-of-tune about micro-movements are more prone to getting caught off-guard by other drivers and their driving behaviors.

Some AI developers would say that detecting micro-movements won't matter in a world of entirely AI self-driving cars, since the AI self-driving cars will presumably all be electronically communicating with each other via V2V (vehicle-to-vehicle) communications. As such, in my example of being at a red light and making a turn, if I was in an AI self-driving car it would have in-theory sent a message to the eager beaver AI self-driving car behind me, and warned it that my AI self-driving car might opt to surge ahead and yet might also then hit the brakes, all because of trying to gauge the traffic situation.

Yes, it is hopefully going to be the case that in an AI self-driving car world we'll see that kind of V2V taking place, but meanwhile we are all living here in the real-world. As I earlier pointed out, for quite some time we are going to have a mix of human driven cars and AI self-driving cars. Likely a long time.

We cannot decide now to avoid putting in place capabilities that involve dealing with human drivers. Pretending that everything will be fine once we get to an all AI self-driving car world, if we ever do, it's living in a dream world. AI self-driving cars must be realistic and deal with a world of human driven cars.

If you take a look at many of the AI self-driving cars being tested on our roadways today, you can often figure out that they aren't using micro-movements to their advantage. The stilted nature of the AI driving is a giveaway that the AI is not versed in detecting, analyzing, and making use of the "tell" of human drivers making micro-movements. In a sense, it is akin to a novice teenage driver that has not yet figured out how to "read" other cars and the driving behaviors of other drivers.

Now, there are some AI developers that claim they are worried that if they do include the detection and leveraging of human drivers' micro-movements that the AI will then potentially get confused or make worse decisions.

Well, this really is more about how good or how poorly the AI development of this feature is undertaken. Sure, if you do a half-baked job of trying to leverage micro-movement detection, you might indeed have your AI self-driving car do worse than if you did things the right way. In my view, that would seem true about any of the capabilities you might opt to include into the AI system. Capabilities that are inadequately put together can be a burden and a problem, more so than an aid and a solution.

I didn't say that adding the capability was going to be easy. In fact, I'll readily state that it is hard.

Trying to use the sensors of an AI self-driving car to detect that the wheels of a car ahead are slightly askew, it's not easy, and you need really good sensors and really good sensor processing software. The same can be said about detecting when nearly any of the typical micro-movements are undertaken.

By definition, those movements are subtle. Picking up on the cues or tells of other cars is hard for other human drivers to do, and admittedly hard for an AI system to do.

Fortunately, you can leverage Machine Learning and Deep Learning to your advantage. By training a deep or large-scale multi-layer artificial neural network with tons of collected driving related data, based on human driven cars as they are driving in regular human driving traffic, there are patterns of the micro-movement driving that can be trained for.

These trained beforehand Machine Learning and Deep Learning algorithms can then be included into the on-board AI system of the self-driving car. In many respects, this is really just a deeper form of those capabilities. The odds are that Machine Learning and Deep Learning are already being used to examine sensory data for aspects such as street signs, the presence of pedestrians, etc. The micro-movements are essentially a step deeper into that kind of analysis.

As mentioned earlier, there are some tough aspects about trying to achieve the inclusion of the micro-movement analysis and usage capability. Will the cameras provide sufficient visual detection to spot the micro-movement? Will the radar provide sufficient detection? Will the LIDAR provide sufficient detection. Also, even if you can get the sensory data, what about the added computer processing needed to go deeply into the analysis, will that be on-board? Does that add cost, weight, heat, or other concerns in terms of providing the AI self-driving car with this capability?

You also need to realize that the micro-movement is not merely about detection. Once you've detected a micro-movement, it needs to be populated into the AI virtual world model. The AI action planner has to be then be versed in what to do with the indications about the micro-movements. If the AI action planner ignores the micro-movement detection, the whole effort is for naught.

The AI action planner also has to deal with micro-movements that might not be a true tell per se.

Recall that I earlier mentioned that in poker playing you might be mistaken about someone's tell. Perhaps you thought that every time they rubbed their cards with their left hand that it meant they were bluffing, but maybe that's not a consistent tell at all. Just because a car ahead of you might be leaning toward the bike lane, it doesn't necessarily mean that the car driver is going to bust into the bike lane.

In this case, the AI needs to be able to include the micro-movements as part of a larger picture or "understanding" of what is happening in the traffic around the AI self-driving car. You cannot in isolation try to make use of the micro-movements. When you are behind another car, you might have several minutes to observe any of their micro-movements. By giving ample time to do so, their pattern of driving behavior is likely going to be more apparent than trying to make a snap judgement.

It is also important to realize that human drivers are going to try and spoof or prank AI self-driving cars. This has already happened in instances of four-way stops, involving human drivers that "intimidated" an AI self-driving car by rolling through the stop sign. The AI was trained to wait until the other drivers came to a full stop. It was the proper way to do things. Human drivers though aren't necessarily "proper" about how they drive. In the four-way stop, the humans figured out that the AI self-driving car would remain still until the human driven cars had waited their turn, and so the human drivers just kept moving, essentially causing the AI self-driving car to freeze in place and continuously wait for its turn to go.

I mention this example of the four-way stop to also point out that the interpretation of micro-movements of human drivers could be a means for human drivers to trick the AI self-driving car.

If you as a human driver know that the AI is going to watch the alignment of your wheels, you could do a kind of basketball-like head fake and shift the direction of your wheels. It might not be due to actually needing to turn the wheels, but instead a ploy to get the AI to perhaps grant you that sought for parking spot or otherwise give you an advantage over the AI system that's driving the self-driving car.

Overall, I am an advocate of including the detection, analysis, and leveraging of human driving micro-movements for the AI to be able to do a better job of driving a self-driving car. It isn't going to be easy to include this capability. It will though make for a more life-like AI driving system and one that since it is going to be immersed among human drivers could be considered an essential driving skill.

When I aided my children in learning to drive, I made sure to explicitly point out the micro-movement's aspects. I'm sure that many parents don't think about it and aren't aware to bring it up for their novice driver children and assume that the kids will somehow just pick it up on their own. There are some AI developers that seem to think the same might happen for AI self-driving cars, namely that rather than trying to overtly train the AI to be mindful of micro-movements, those AI developers hope or assume that it will somehow emerge by the AI's own divinity. I doubt it will.

I've tried to answer the first question which was whether or not AI self-driving cars should be outfitted with a capability to detect, analyze, and leverage the micro-movements made by human drivers. Of course, I said yes.

The second question that I get asked is whether the AI self-driving car should make use of micro-movements, doing so in a similar manner to how human drivers use micro-movements.

My answer is yes, the AI ought to also make use of micro-movements. Here's why.

Human drivers are generally used to detecting the micro-movements of other cars. I realize that I've also given examples of human drivers that seem oblivious to detecting micro-movements, but those are a smaller percentage of drivers.

I would also claim that many drivers might not be consciously aware that they are being affected by the micro-movements of other drivers, and yet they are indeed being impacted. You might catch out of the corner of your eye, the subtle micro-movement of another car. Doing so, you might react without any recognizable or spoken aloud reason and respond to that micro-movement, nonetheless. Humans are quite good at doing pattern matching. They often are able to find patterns when they aren't even thinking explicitly about doing so.

An AI self-driving car should be sending the same kind of subtle "signals" to human drivers, doing akin to what other human drivers do. This again is part of my overarching belief that if AI self-driving cars are going to be driving among human drivers, which we know to be the case, those AI drivers need to be doing actions that human drivers do.

If the AI lacks the micro-movement showcase capability, it means that those human drivers around the AI self-driving car will no longer have an essential "tell" that can forecast what the AI self-driving car is going to do. Without the tell, the human drivers are going to be caught unawares. What, that stupid darned AI self-driving car made a right turn, I wasn't expecting it, will be a common complaint.

And in a manner of speaking, I'd say that those human drivers will be right. They will be well-justified in their complaining. Who wants to have other drivers (human or AI), for which those drivers do things seemingly without the usual warnings (or tells) that we already have grown accustomed to seeing? It's a recipe for disaster.

Would you be willing to put onto our roadways a slew of drivers that aren't driving as is customary? Not a good move.

If you did so, it would be like dividing the traffic into two classes of drivers. When you combine with this that the human drivers won't readily be able to gauge what the AI driver is going to do, and if the AI driver isn't also versed in reading micro-movements and therefore unaware of what the human driver is going to do, you are setting things up for a very messy and untoward outcome.

Conclusion

I sometimes liken the micro-movements topic to the nature of dancing. If two people are going to dance together, they need to figure out the subtle movements that indicate whether to turn to the left or turn to the right, and whether to speed-up or slow down the pace.

Each dancer needs to be able to detect the micro-movements of the other, along with knowing how to react.

Furthermore, each dancer needs to be able to exhibit their own micro-movements, in order to allow their dancing partner to detect the movement and be able to react accordingly.

Right now, we have humans that detect the micro-movements of other human drivers, plus human drivers emit micro-movements as part of their driving efforts (by-and-large). We are in the midst of witnessing AI self-driving cars being fielded and tested that don't detect the micro-movements of other cars, and nor do the AI self-driving cars emit their own micro-movements.

You can't have much of a fluid dance when one of the partners is clueless. In the case of cars, a dance partner that is clueless can lead to untoward car accidents.

Human drivers won't judge what the AI is going to do, and bang, there will be collisions. AI self-driving cars won't be able to well-judge what human drivers are going to do, and as a result the AI will drive in an overly timid and hesitant way, which will likely ultimately lead to car accidents.

It's time to make sure that the dancing partners of human drivers and AI drivers are versed in the same kinds of capabilities and tactics of driving. I vote that the auto makers and tech firms put more effort toward the micro-movement elements, which makes sense to ensure that the dancing partners won't collide into each other and make ghastly missteps.

CHAPTER 5

BOEING 737 ASPECTS AND AI SELF-DRIVING CARS

CHAPTER 5
BOEING 737 ASPECTS AND AI SELF-DRIVING CARS

The Boeing 737 MAX 8 aircraft has been in the news recently, doing so sadly as a result of a fatal crash that occurred on March 10, 2019 involving Ethiopian Airlines flight #302.

News reports suggest that another fatal crash of the Boeing 737 MAX 8 that took place on October 29, 2018 for Lion Air flight #610 might be similar in terms of how the March 10, 2019 crash took place. It is noteworthy to point out that the Lion Air crash is still under investigation, possibly with a final report being released later this year, and the Ethiopian Airlines crash investigation is just now starting (at the time of this writing).

I'd like to consider at this stage of understanding about the crashes whether we can tentatively identify aspects about the matter that could be instructive toward the design, development, testing, and fielding of Artificial Intelligence (AI) systems.

Though the Boeing 737 MAX 8 does not include elements that might be considered in the AI bailiwick per se, it seems relatively apparent that systems underlying the aircraft could be likened to how advanced automation is utilized. Perhaps the Boeing 737 MAX 8 incidents can reveal vital and relevant characteristics that can be valuable insights for AI systems, especially AI systems of a real-time nature.

A modern-day aircraft is outfitted with a variety of complex automated systems that need to operate on a real-time basis. During the course of a flight, starting even when the aircraft is on the ground and getting ready for flight, there are a myriad of systems that must each play a part in the motion and safety of the plane. Furthermore, these systems are at times either under the control of the human pilots or are in a sense co-sharing the flying operations with the human pilots. The Human Machine Interface (HMI) is a key matter to the co-sharing arrangement.

I'm going to concentrate my relevancy depiction on a particular type of real-time AI system, namely AI self-driving cars.

Please though do not assume that the insights or lessons mentioned herein are only applicable to AI self-driving cars. I would assert that the points made are equally important for other real-time AI systems, such as robots that are working in a factory or warehouse, and of course other AI autonomous vehicles such as drones and submersibles. You can even take out of the equation the real-time aspects and consider that these points still would readily apply to AI systems that are considered less-than real-time in their activities.

One overarching aspect that I'd like to put clearly onto the table is that this discussion is not about the Boeing 737 MAX 8 as to the actual legal underpinnings of the aircraft and the crashes. I am not trying to solve the question of what happened in those crashes. I am not trying to analyze the details of the Boeing 737 MAX 8. Those kinds of analyzes are still underway and by experts that are versed in the particulars of airplanes and that are closely examining the incidents. That's not what this is about herein.

I am going to instead try to surface out of the various media reporting the semblance of what some seem to believe might have taken place. Those media guesses might be right, they might be wrong. Time will tell. What I want to do is see whether we can turn the murkiness into something that might provide helpful tips and suggestions of what can or might someday or already is happening in AI systems.

I realize that some of you might argue that it is premature to be "unpacking" the incidents. Shouldn't we wait until the final reports are released? Again, I am not wanting to make assertions about what did or did not actually happen. Among the many and varied theories and postulations, I believe there is a richness of insights that can be right now applied to how we are approaching the design, development, testing, and fielding of AI systems. I'd also claim that time is of the essence, meaning that it would behoove those AI efforts already underway to be thinking about the points I'll be bringing up.

Allow me to fervently clarify that the points I'll raise are not dependent on how the investigations bear out about the Boeing 737 MAX 8 incidents. Instead, my points are at a level of abstraction that they are useful for AI systems efforts, regardless of what the final reporting says about the flight crashes. That being said, it could very well be that the flight crash investigations undercover other and additional useful points, all of which could further be applied to how we think about and approach AI systems.

As you read herein the brief recap about the flight crashes and the aircraft, allow yourself the latitude that we don't yet know what really happened. Therefore, the discussion is by-and-large of a tentative nature.

New facts are likely to emerge. Viewpoints might change over time. In any case, I'll try to repeatedly state that the aspects being described are tentative and you should refrain from judging those aspects, allowing your mind to focus on how the points can be used for enhancing AI systems.

Even something that turns out to not have been true in the flight crashes can nonetheless still present a possibility of something that could have happened, and for which we can leverage that understanding to the advantage of AI systems adoption.

So, do not trample on this discussion because you find something amiss about a characterization of the aircraft and/or the incident. Look past any such transgression. Consider whether the points surfaced can be helpful to AI developers and to those organizations embarking upon crafting AI systems. That's what this is about.

Background About the Boeing 737 MAX 8

The Boeing 737 was first flown in late 1960's and spawned a multitude of variants over the years, including in the 1990s the Boeing 737 NG (Next Generation) series. Considered the most selling aircraft for commercial flight, last year the Boeing 737 model surpassed sales of 10,000 units sold. It is composed of twin jets, a relatively narrow body, and intended for a flight range of short to medium distances. The successor to the NG series is the Boeing 737 MAX series.

As part of the family of Boeing 737's, the MAX series is based on the prior 737 designs and was purposely re-engined by Boeing, along with having changes made to the aerodynamics and the airframe, doing so to make key improvements including a lowered burn rate of fuel and other aspects that would make the plane more efficient and have a longer range than its prior versions. The initial approval to proceed with the Boeing 737 MAX series was signified by the Boeing board of directors in August 2011.

Per many news reports, there were discussions within Boeing about whether to start anew and craft a brand-new design for the Boeing 737 MAX series or whether to continue and retrofit the design. The decision was made to retrofit the prior design.

Of the changes made to prior designs, perhaps the most notable element consisted of mounting the engines further forward and higher than had been done for prior models. This design change tended to have an upward pitching effect on the plane. It was more so prone to this than prior versions, as a result of the more powerful engines being used (having greater thrust capacity) and the positioning at a higher and more pronounced forward position on the aircraft.

As to a possibility of the Boeing 737 MAX entering into a potential stall during flight due to this retrofitted approach, particularly doing so in a situation where the flaps are retracted and at low-speed and with a nose-up condition, the retrofit design added a new system called the MCAS (Maneuvering Characteristics Augmentation System).

The MCAS is essentially software that receives sensor data and then based on the readings will attempt to trim down the nose in an effort to avoid having the plane get into a dangerous nose-up stall during flight. This is considered a stall prevention system.

The primary sensor used by the MCAS consists of an AOA (Angle of Attack) sensor, which is a hardware device mounted on the plane and transmits data within the plane, including feeding of the data to the MCAS system. In many respects, the AOA is a relatively simple kind of sensor and variants of AOA's in term of brands, models, and designs exist on most modern-day airplanes. This is to point out that there is nothing unusual per se about the use of AOA sensors, it is a common practice to use AOA sensors.

Algorithms used in the MCAS were intended to try and ascertain whether the plane might be in a dangerous condition as based on the AOA data being reported and in conjunction with the airspeed and altitude. If the MCAS software calculated what was considered a dangerous condition, the MCAS would then activate to fly the plane so that the nose would be brought downward to try and obviate the dangerous upward-nose potential-stall condition.

The MCAS was devised such that it would automatically activate to fly the plane based on the AOA readings and based on its own calculations about a potentially dangerous condition. This activation occurs without notifying the human pilot and is considered an automatic engagement.

Note that the human pilot does not overtly act to engage the MCAS per se, instead the MCAS is essentially always on and detecting whether it should engage or not (unless the human pilot opts to entirely turn it off).

During a MCAS engagement, if a human pilot tries to trim the plane and uses a switch on the yoke to do so, the MCAS becomes temporarily disengaged. In a sense, the human pilot and the MCAS automated system are co-sharing the flight controls. This is an important point since the MCAS is still considered active and ready to re-engage on its own.

A human pilot can entirely disengage the MCAS and turn it off, if the human pilot believes that turning off the MCAS activation is warranted. It is not difficult to turn off the MCAS, though it presumably would rarely if ever be turned off and might be considered an extraordinary and seldom action that would be undertaken by a pilot. Since the MCAS is considered an essential element of the plane, turning off the MCAS would be a serious act and not be done without presumably the human pilot considering the tradeoffs in doing so.

In the case of the Lion Air crash, one theory is that shortly after taking off the MCAS might have attempted to push down the nose and that the human pilots were simultaneously trying to pull-up the nose, perhaps being unaware that the MCAS was trying to push down the nose. This appears to account for a roller coaster up-and-down effort that the plane seemed to experience. Some have pointed out that a human pilot might believe they have a stabilizer trim issue, referred to as a runaway stabilizer or runaway trim, and misconstrue a situation in which the MCAS is engaged and acting on the stabilizer trim.

Speculation based on that theory is that the human pilot did not realize they were in a sense fighting with the MCAS to control the plane, and had the human pilot realized what was actually happening, it would have been relatively easy to have turned off the MCAS and taken over control of the plane, no longer being in a co-sharing mode. There have been documented cases of other pilots turning off the MCAS when they believed that it was fighting against their efforts to control the Boeing 737 MAX 8.

One aspect that according to news reports is somewhat murky involves the AOA sensors in the case of the Lion Air incident. Some suggest that there was only one AOA sensor on the airplane and that it fed to the MCAS faulty data, leading the MCAS to push the nose down, even though apparently or presumably a nose down effort was not actually warranted.

Other reports say that there were two AOA sensors, one on the Captain's side of the plane and one on the other side, and that the AOA on the Captains side generated faulty readings while the one on the other side was generating proper readings, and that the MCAS apparently ignored the properly functioning AOA and instead accepted the faulty readings coming from the Captain's side.

There are documented cases of AOA sensors at times becoming faulty. One aspect too is that environmental conditions can impact the AOA sensor. If there is build-up of water or ice on the AOA sensor, it can impact the sensor. Keep in mind that there are a variety of AOA sensors in terms of brands and models, thus, not all AOA sensors are necessarily going to have the same capabilities and limitations.

The first commercial flights of the Boeing 737 MAX 8 took place in May 2017. There are other models of the Boeing 737 MAX series, both ones existing and ones envisioned, including the MAX 7, the MAX 8, the MAX 9, etc. In the case of the Lion Air incident, which occurred in October 2018, it was the first fatal incident of the Boeing 737 MAX series.

There are a slew of other aspects about the Boeing 737 MAX 8 and the incidents, and if interested you can readily find such information online. The recap that I've provided does not cover all facets -- I have focused on key elements that I'd like to next discuss with regard to AI systems.

Shifting Hats to AI Self-Driving Cars Topic

Let's shift hats for a moment and discuss some background about AI self-driving cars. Once I've done so, I'll then dovetail together the insights that might be gleaned about the Boeing 737 MAX 8 aspects and how this can potentially be useful when designing, building, testing, and fielding AI self-driving cars.

At the Cybernetic AI Self-Driving Car Institute, we are developing AI software for self-driving cars. As such, we are quite interested in whatever lessons can be learned from other advanced automation development efforts and seek to apply those lessons to our efforts, and I'm sure that the auto makers and tech firms also developing AI self-driving car systems are keenly interested in too.

I'd like to first clarify and introduce the notion that there are varying levels of AI self-driving cars. The topmost level is considered Level 5. A Level 5 self-driving car is one that is being driven by the AI and there is no human driver involved. For the design of Level 5 self-driving cars, the auto makers are even removing the gas pedal, brake pedal, and steering wheel, since those are contraptions used by human drivers. The Level 5 self-driving car is not being driven by a human and nor is there an expectation that a human driver will be present in the self-driving car. It's all on the shoulders of the AI to drive the car.

For self-driving cars less than a Level 5, there must be a human driver present in the car. The human driver is currently considered the responsible party for the acts of the car. The AI and the human driver are co-sharing the driving task. In spite of this co-sharing, the human is supposed to remain fully immersed into the driving task and be ready at all times to perform the driving task.

I've repeatedly warned about the dangers of this co-sharing arrangement and predicted it will produce many untoward results.

Let's focus herein on the true Level 5 self-driving car. Much of the comments apply to the less than Level 5 self-driving cars too, but the fully autonomous AI self-driving car will receive the most attention in this discussion.

Here's the usual steps involved in the AI driving task:

- Sensor data collection and interpretation
- Sensor fusion
- Virtual world model updating
- AI action planning
- Car controls command issuance

Another key aspect of AI self-driving cars is that they will be driving on our roadways in the midst of human driven cars too. There are some pundits of AI self-driving cars that continually refer to a utopian world in which there are only AI self-driving cars on the public roads. Currently there are about 250+ million conventional cars in the United States alone, and those cars are not going to magically disappear or become true Level 5 AI self-driving cars overnight.

Indeed, the use of human driven cars will last for many years, likely many decades, and the advent of AI self-driving cars will occur while there are still human driven cars on the roads. This is a crucial point since this means that the AI of self-driving cars needs to be able to contend with not just other AI self-driving cars, but also contend with human driven cars.

It is easy to envision a simplistic and rather unrealistic world in which all AI self-driving cars are politely interacting with each other and being civil about roadway interactions. That's not what is going to be happening for the foreseeable future. AI self-driving cars and human driven cars will need to be able to cope with each other.

Returning to the matter of the Boeing 737 MAX 8, let's consider some potential insights that can be gleaned from what the news has been reporting.

Here's a list of the points I'm going to cover:

- Retrofit versus start anew
- Single sensor versus multiple sensors reliance
- Sensor fusion calculations
- Human Machine Interface (HMI) designs
- Education/training of human operators
- Cognitive dissonance and Theory of Mind
- Testing of complex systems
- Firms and their development teams
- Safety considerations for advanced systems

I'll cover each of the points, doing so by first reminding you of my recap about the Boeing 737 MAX 8 as it relates to the point being made, and then shifting into a focus on AI systems and especially AI self-driving cars for that point.

I've opted to number the points to make them easier to refer to as a sequence of points, but the sequence number does not denote any kind of priority of one point being more or less important than another. They are all worthy points.

Take a look at Figure 1.

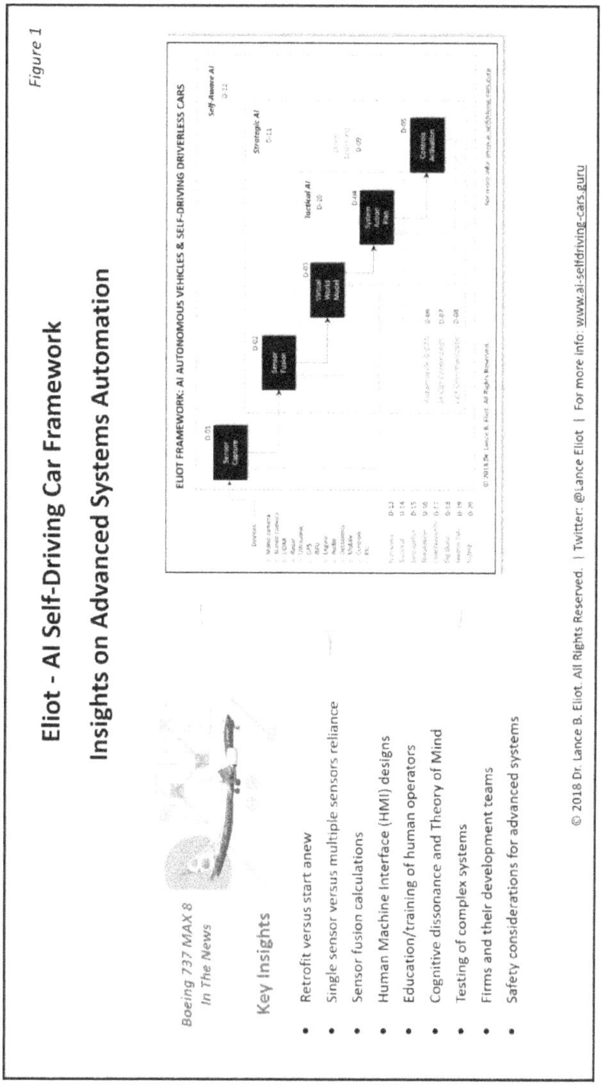
Figure 1
Eliot - AI Self-Driving Car Framework
Insights on Advanced Systems Automation
Boeing 737 MAX 8
In The News
ELIOT FRAMEWORK: AI AUTONOMOUS VEHICLES & SELF-DRIVING DRIVERLESS CARS
Sensor Capture
Sensor Fusion
Virtual World Model
System Action Plan
Controls Activation
Tactical AI
Strategic AI
Self-Aware AI
Key Insights
• Retrofit versus start anew
• Single sensor versus multiple sensors reliance
• Sensor fusion calculations
• Human Machine Interface (HMI) designs
• Education/training of human operators
• Cognitive dissonance and Theory of Mind
• Testing of complex systems
• Firms and their development teams
• Safety considerations for advanced systems
© 2018 Dr. Lance B. Eliot. All Rights Reserved. | Twitter: @Lance Eliot | For more info: www.ai-selfdriving-cars.guru

Key Point #1: Retrofit versus start anew

Recall that the Boeing 737 MAX 8 is a retrofit of prior designs of the Boeing 737. Some have suggested that the "problem" being solved by the MCAS is a problem that should never have existed at all, namely that rather than creating an issue by adding the more powerful engines and putting them further forward and higher, perhaps the plane ought to have been redesigned entirely anew. Those that make this suggestion are then assuming that the stall prevention capability of the MCAS would not have been needed, which then would have not been built into the planes, which then would never have led to a human pilot essentially co-sharing and battling with it to fly the plane.

Don't know. Might there have been a need for an MCAS anyway? In any case, let's not get mired in that aspect about the Boeing 737 MAX 8 herein.

Instead, think about AI systems and the question of whether to retrofit an existing AI system or start anew.

You might be tempted to believe that AI self-driving cars are so new that they are entirely a new design anyway. This is not quite correct. There are some AI self-driving car efforts that have built upon prior designs and are continually "retrofitting" a prior design, doing so by extending, enhancing, and otherwise leveraging the prior foundation.

This makes sense in that starting from scratch is going to be quite an endeavor. If you have something that already seems to work, and if you can adjust it to make it better, you would likely be able to do so at a lower cost and at a faster pace of development.

One consideration is whether the prior design might have issues that you are not aware of and are perhaps carrying those into the retrofitted version. That's not good.

Another consideration is whether the effort to retrofit requires changes that introduce new problems that were not previously in the prior design. This emphasizes that the retrofit changes are not necessarily always of an upbeat nature. You can make alterations that lead to new issues, which then require you to presumably craft new solutions, and those new solutions are "new" and therefore not already well-tested via prior designs.

I routinely forewarn AI self-driving car auto makers and tech firms to be cautious as they continue to build upon prior designs. It is not necessarily pain free.

Key Point #2: Single sensor versus multiple sensors reliance

For the Boeing 737 MAX 8, I've mentioned that there are the AOA (Angle of Attack) sensors and they play a crucial role in the MCAS system. It's not entirely clear whether there is just one AOA or two of the AOA sensors involved in the matter, but in any case, it seems like the AOA is the only type of sensor involved for that particular purpose, though presumably there must be other sensors such as registering the height and speed of the plane that are encompassed by the data feed going into the MCAS.

Let's though assume for the moment that the AOA is the only sensor for what it does on the plane, namely ascertaining the angle of attack of the plane. Go with me on this assumption, though I don't know for sure if it is true.

The reason I bring up this aspect is that if you have an advanced system that is dependent upon only one kind of sensor to provide a crucial indication of the physical aspects of the system, you might be painting yourself into an uncomfortable corner. In the case of AI self-driving cars, suppose that we used only cameras for detecting the surroundings of the self-driving car. It means that the rest of the AI self-driving car system is solely dependent upon whether the cameras are working properly and whether the vision processing systems is working correctly.

If we add to the AI self-driving car another capability, such as radar sensors, we now have a means to double-check the cameras. We could add another capability such as LIDAR, and we'd have a triple check involved. We could add ultrasonic sensors too. And so on.

Now, we must realize that the more sensors you add, the more the cost goes up, along with the complexity of the system rising too.

For each added sensor type, you need to craft an entire capability around it, including where to position the sensors, how to connect them into the rest of the system, and having the software that can collect the sensor data and interpret it. There is added weight to the self-driving car, there is added power consumption being consumed, there is more heat generated by the sensors, etc. Also, the amount of computer processing required goes up, including the number of processors, the memory needed, and the like.

You cannot just start including more sensors because you think it will be handy to have them on the self-driving car. Each added sensor involves a lot of added effort and costs. There is an ROI (Return on Investment) involved in making such decisions. I've stated many times in my writings and presentations whether Elon Musk and Tesla's decision to not use LIDAR is going to ultimately backfire on them, and even Elon Musk himself has said it might.

I'd like to then use the AOA matter as a wake-up call about the kinds of sensors that the auto makers and tech firms are putting onto their AI self-driving cars. Do you have a type of sensor for which no other sensor can obtain something similar? If so, are you ready to handle the possibility that if the sensor goes bad, your AI system is going to be in the blind about what is happening, or perhaps worse still that it will get faulty readings.

This does bring up another handy point, specifically how to cope with a sensor that is being faulty.

The AI system cannot assume that a sensor is always going to be working properly. The "easiest" kind of problem is when the sensor fails entirely, and the AI system gets no readings from it at all. I say this is easiest in that the AI then can pretty much make a reasonable assumption that the sensor is then dead and no longer to be relied upon. This doesn't mean that handling the self-driving car is "easy" and it only means that at least the AI kind of knows that the sensor is not working.

The tricky part is when a sensor becomes faulty but has not entirely failed. This is a scary gray area. The AI might not realize that the sensor is faulty and therefore assume that everything the sensor is reporting must be correct and accurate.

Suppose a camera is having problems and it is occasionally ghosting images, meaning that an image sent to the AI system has shown perhaps cars that aren't really there or pedestrians that aren't really there. This could be disastrous. The rest of the AI might suddenly jam on the brakes to avoid a pedestrian, someone that's not actually there in front of the self-driving car. Or, maybe the self-driving car is unable to detect a pedestrian in the street because the camera is faulting and sending images that have omissions.

The sensor and the AI system must have a means to try and ascertain whether the sensor is faulting or not. It could be that the sensor itself is having a physical issue, maybe by wear-and-tear or maybe it was hit or bumped by some other matter such as the self-driving car nudging another car. Another strong possibility for most sensors is the chance of it getting covered up by dirt, mud, snow, and other environmental aspects. The sensor itself is still functioning but it cannot get solid readings due to the obstruction.

AI self-driving car makers need to be thoughtfully and carefully considering how their sensors operate and what they can do to detect faulty conditions, along with either trying to correct for the faulty readings or at least inform and alert the rest of the AI system that faultiness is happening. This is serious stuff. Unfortunately, sometimes it is given short shrift.

Key Point #3: Sensor fusion calculations

As mentioned earlier, one theory was that the Boeing 737 MAX 8 in the Lion Air incident had two AOA sensors and one of the sensors was faulting, while the other sensor was still good, and yet the MCAS supposedly opted to ignore the good sensor and instead rely upon the faulty one.

In the case of AI self-driving cars, an important aspect involves undertaking a kind of sensor fusion to figure out a larger overall notion of what is happening with the self-driving car. The sensor fusion subsystem needs to collect together the sensory data or perhaps the sensory interpretations from the myriad of sensors and try to reconcile them. Doing so is handy because each type of sensor might be seeing the world from a particular viewpoint, and by "triangulating" the various sensors, the AI system can derive a more holistic understanding of the traffic around the self-driving car.

Would it be possible for an AI self-driving car to opt to rely upon a faulting sensor and simultaneously ignore or downplay a fully functioning sensor? Yes, absolutely, it could happen.

It all depends upon how the sensor fusion was design and developed to work. If the AI developers though that say the forward camera is more reliable overall than the forward radar, they might have developed the software such that it tends to weight the camera more so than the radar. This can mean that when the sensor fusion is trying to decide which sensor to choose as providing the right indication at the time, it might default to the camera, rather than the radar, even if the camera is in a faulting mode.

Perhaps the sensor fusion is unaware that the camera is faulting, and so it gives the benefit of the doubt to the camera. Or, maybe the sensor fusion realizes the camera is faulting, but it has been setup to nonetheless choose the camera over the radar, rightfully or wrongly.

The decisions made by the AI developers are going to pretty much determine what happens during the sensor fusion. If the design is not fully baked, or if the design was not implemented as intended, you can definitely end-up with situations that seem oddball from a logical perspective.

This point highlights the importance of designing the sensor fusion in a manner that best leverages the myriad of sensors, along with having extensive error checking and correcting, along with being able to deal with good and bad sensors. This includes the troublesome and at times hard to figure out intermittent faulting of a sensor.

Key Point #4: Human Machine Interface (HMI) designs

According to the news reports, the MCAS is automatically always activated and trying to figure out whether it should engage into the act of co-sharing the flight controls. It seems that some pilots of the aircraft might not realize this is the case. Perhaps some are unaware of the MCAS, or maybe some are aware of the MCAS but believe that it will only engage at their human piloting directive to do so.

Besides this always-on aspect, perhaps there are some human pilots that don't know how to turn-off the feature, or they might have once known and have forgotten how to do so. Or, maybe while in the midst of a crisis, they aren't considering whether the MCAS could be erroneously fighting them and therefore it doesn't occur to them to disengage it entirely.

They might also during a crisis be trying to consider a wide variety of possibilities of what is happening to the plane. From a hindsight viewpoint, maybe it is easy to isolate the MCAS and for someone to say that it was the culprit, but in the midst of a moment when the plane is fighting against you, your mental effort is devoted to trying to right the plane, along with seeking reasons for why the plane is having troubles. There is a potential large mental search space that the human pilot has to analyze, and yet this is happening in real-time with obvious serious and life-or-death consequences involved.

What makes this seemingly even more subtle in the case of the MCAS is that it apparently will temporarily disengage when the pilot uses the yoke switch, but the MCAS will then re-engage when it calculates that there is need to do so. A human pilot might at first believe that they've disengaged entirely the MCAS, when all that's happened is that it has temporarily disengaged. When the MCAS re-engages, the human pilot could be baffled as to why the control is once again having troubles.

Combine this on-and-off kind of automatic action with the throes of dealing with the plane in a crisis mode. You've got a confluence of factors that can begin to overwhelm the human pilot. It can be difficult for them to sort out what is actually taking place. They meanwhile will continue to do what seems the proper course of action, bring up the nose. Ironically, this is seemingly likely to get the MCAS to once again step into the co-sharing and try to push down the nose.

I'd like to do a quick thought experiment on this.

Imagine a car with two sets of steering wheels and pedals. We'll put those driving controls in the front seats of the car. Let's also place a barrier between the driver's seat and the second driver that we'll say is just to the right of the normal position for a driver. The barrier is sizable and masks the actions of the other driver.

The driver in the normal driving position is asked to drive the car. They do so. Suppose they drive it a lot, so much that after a while they kind of forget that a second driver is sitting next to them (hidden from view by the barrier).

At one point, the car starts to get into trouble and appears to be sliding out of the lane. The second driver, the one that has been silent and not doing anything so far, other than watching the road, decides they need to step into the driving effort and correct the sliding aspects. The first driver, having gotten used to driving the car themselves, and having no overt awareness that the second driver is now going to operate the controls, believes they are the only driver of the car.

The two drivers begin fighting with each other in terms of working the driving controls, yet neither of them seems to realize that the other driver is doing so. They are seemingly working in isolation of each other, though they both have their "hands" on the controls.

You might exclaim that the second driver should be telling the first driver that they are now working the driving controls. Hey you, over there on the other side of the barrier, I'm trying to keep you from sliding out of the lane, might be a handy thing to say. If there is no particular communication taking place between the two, they might not realize how they are each countering the other, and possibly making the situation worse and worse in doing so.

I've many times exhorted that in the case of AI self-driving cars we are heading into untoward territory as the AI gets more advanced and yet does not entirely drive the car itself. In the case of Level 3 self-driving cars, there is going to be a struggle of the human driver and the AI system in terms of co-sharing the driving task. In some ways, my thought experiment highlights what can happen.

That's why some AI self-driving car makers are trying to jump past Level 3 and go straight to Level 4 and Level 5. Others are determined to proceed with Level 3. It's going to be a question of whether human drivers fully grasp what they are supposed to do versus what the AI system is supposed to do.

Will the human driver understand what the Level 3 capabilities are? Will the human driver know that the AI is trying to drive the car? Will the AI realize when the human opts to drive the car? Will the AI realize that a human driver is actually ready and able to drive the car? When a crisis moment arises, such as the AI is driving the car at 60 miles per hour and suddenly determines that it has reached a point where the human driver ought to takeover the controls, this is a dicey proposition. Is the human driver prepared to do so, and do they know why the AI has determined it is time to have the human drive the car?

Much of this center on the Human Machine Interface (HMI) aspects.

When you are co-sharing the driving, both parties have to be properly and timely informed about what the other party is doing or wants to do or wants the other party to do. For a car, this might be done via indicators that light-up on the dashboard, or maybe the AI system speaks to the driver.

This though is not a straightforward aspect to arrange for all circumstances.

For example, if the AI speaks to the driver and explains that the driver needs to take over the wheel, imagine how long it takes for the speaking to occur, along with the driver having to make sure they are listening, and that they heard what the AI said, and that they comprehend what the AI said.

This then also requires time for the human to consider what action they should take, and then take that action. This is precious time when there is a crisis moment and driving decisions need to be quickly made and enacted.

Key Point #5: Education/training of human operators

One question that is being asked about the Boeing 737 MAX 8 situation involves how much education or training should be provided to the human pilots, in particular related to the MCAS, and overall how the human pilots were or are to be made aware of the MCAS facets.

In the case of AI self-driving cars, one obvious difference between driving a car and flying a plane is that the airplane pilots are working in a professional capacity, while a human driving a car is generally doing so in a more informal manner (I'll exclude for the moment professional drivers such as race car drivers, taxi drivers, shuttle drivers, etc.).

Commercial airline pilots are governed by all kinds of rules about education, training, number of hours flying, certification, re-certification, and the like. I'm not going to dig further into the MCAS education and training aspects, and so let's just consider what kind of education or training you might have for dealing with an advanced automation that is co-sharing the driving task with you.

For today's everyday licensed driver of a car, I think we can all agree that they get a somewhat minimal amount of education and training about driving a car. This though seems to have worked out relatively okay, since most drivers most of the time seem to be able to sufficiently operate a normal car.

Part of the reason that we have been able to keep the amount of education and training relatively low for driving a car is because of the amazing simplicity of driving a conventional car. You need to know how to operate the brakes, the accelerator, the steering wheel, and how to put the car into gear. The rest of the driving task is about ascertaining where you are driving and then performing the tactical aspects of driving, such as speeding up, slowing down, and steering in one direction or another.

When you get a car, there is usually an owner's manual that indicates the specifics of that brand and model of a car. Still, for a conventional car, there isn't that much new to deal with. The pedals are still in the same places, the steering wheel is still the steering wheel. Switching from one gear to another often differs from car brand to another car brand, yet it doesn't take much to figure this out.

I know many drivers that have no idea how to engage their cruise control. They've never used it on their car. They don't care to use it. I know many drivers that aren't exactly sure how their Anti-lock Braking System (ABS) works, but most of the time it won't matter that they don't know, since it usually automatically works for you.

As the Level 3 self-driving cars begin to appear in the marketplace, one rather looming question will be to what extent should human drivers be educated or trained about what the Level 3 does. In the case of the Tesla models, generally considered a Level 2, we've had drivers that seemed to think they can fall asleep at the wheel when the AutoPilot is engaged. That's not the case. They are still considered the responsible driver of the car.

Things are going to get dicey with the Level 3 systems and the human drivers. They are co-sharing the driving task. Should the human driver of a Level 3 car be required to take a certain amount of education or training on how to operate that Level 3 car? If so, how will this education or training take place? Some pundits say that it can be just done by the salesperson that sells the car, but I think we'd all be a bit suspect about the thoroughness of that kind of training effort.

I've predicted that we will be soon seeing lawsuits against auto makers that might opt to either offer no training for their Level 3 cars, or scant training, or training that is construed as optional and so the human driver later on claims they did not realize the importance of it. Things are going to get messy.

Key Point #6: Cognitive dissonance and Theory of Mind

A human operator of a device or system needs to have in their mind a mental model of what the device or system can and cannot do. If the human operator does not mentally know what the other party can or cannot do, it will make for a rather poor effort of collaboration.

You've likely seen this in human-to-human relationships, whereby you might not have a clear picture in your mind of the other person's capabilities, and therefore it is hard for the two of you to work together in a properly functional manner.

The other day I went bike riding with a colleague. I am used to vigorous bike rides, but I didn't know if he was too. If I had suddenly started riding like the wind, it could have left him behind, along with his becoming confused about what we were doing.

Having a mental picture of the other person's capabilities is often referred to as the Theory of Mind. What is your understanding of the other person's way of thinking? In the case of flying a plane, the question is whether you comprehend what the automation of the plane can and cannot do, along with when it will do so. The same can be said about a car, namely that the human driver needs to understand what a car can and cannot do, and when it will do so.

If there is a mental gap between the understanding of the human operator and the device or system they are operating, it creates a situation of cognitive dissonance. The human operator is likely to fail to take the appropriate actions since they misunderstand what the automation is or has done.

For the MCAS, it would seem that perhaps some of the human pilots might have had an inadequate understanding of the Theory of Mind about what the MCAS was and does. This might have created situations of cognitive dissonance. As such, the human pilot would be unable to gauge what to do about the automation, and how to work with it.

Human drivers in even conventional cars can have the same lack of Theory of Mind about the car and its operations. In the case of having ABS brakes, you are not supposed to pump those brakes when trying to come to a stop, doing so actually tends to have the opposite reaction of your attempting to stop the car quickly. Some human drivers are used to cars that don't have ABS and in those cars you might indeed pump the brakes, but not with ABS. I dare say many human drivers are at a cognitive dissonance about the use of their ABS brakes.

The same kind of cognitive dissonance will be more pronounced with Level 3 cars. Human drivers have a greater hurdle and burden of learning what the Theory of Mind is of their Level 3 cars, and the odds are those human drivers will be unaware of or confused about those features. A potential recipe for disaster.

Key Point #7: Testing of complex systems

There is an ongoing discussion in the media about how the MCAS was tested. I'm not going to venture into the details about that aspect. In any case, it does spark the question of how to test advanced automation systems.

Let's suppose an advanced automation system is tested to make sure that it seems to work as devised. Maybe you do simulations of it. Maybe you do tests in a wind tunnel in the case of avionics systems, or for an AI self-driving car you take it to a proving ground or closed track.

If the tests are solely about whether the system does what was expected, it might pass with flying colors. Did the tests though include what will happen when something goes awry?

Suppose a sensor becomes faulty, what happens then? I've actually had engineers that tell me there was nothing in the specification about a sensor becoming faulty, so they didn't develop anything to handle that aspect, therefore it made no sense to test it for a faulty sensor, since they could already tell you that it wasn't designed and nor programmed to deal with it.

Another kind of test involves the HMI aspects and the human operator.

If the advanced automation is supposed to work hand-in-hand with a human operator, you ought to have tests to see if that really is working out as anticipated. One guffaw that I've often seen involves training the human operator and then immediately doing a test of the system with the human operator. That's handy, but what about a week later when the human operator has forgotten about some of the training? Also, what about a human operator that received little or no training, which I've had engineers tell me that they don't test for that condition since they are told beforehand that all of the human operators will always have the needed training.

Key Point #8: Firms and development teams

Usually, advanced automation systems are designed, developed, tested, and fielded as part of large teams and within overall organizations that shape how these work efforts will be undertaken.

Crucial decisions about the nature of the design are not usually made by one person alone. It is a group effort. There can be compromises along the way. There can be miscommunication about what the design is or will do. The same can happen during the development. And the same can happen during the testing. And the same can happen during the fielding.

My point is that it can be easy to fall into the mental trap of focusing only on the technology itself, whether it is a plane or a self-driving car. You need to also consider the wider context of how the artifact came to be. Was the effort a well-informed and thoughtful approach or did the approach itself lend towards incorporating problems or issues into the resultant outcome.

Key Point #9: Safety considerations for advanced systems

The safety record of today's airplanes is really quite remarkable when you think about it.

This has not happened by chance. There is a tremendous emphasis on flight safety. It gets baked into every step of the design, development, testing, and fielding of an airplane, along with its daily operation. In spite of that top-of-mind about safety, things can still at times go awry.

In the case of AI self-driving cars, I'd suggest that things are not as safety conscious as yet and we need to push further along on becoming more safety aware.

I've urged the auto makers and tech firms to put in place a Chief Safety Officer, charged with making sure that everything that happens when designing, building, testing, and fielding of an AI self-driving car that safety is a key focus.

There are numerous steps to be baked into AI self-driving cars that will increase their safety, without which, I've prophesied we'll see things go south and the AI self-driving car dream might be delayed or dashed.

Conclusion

I've touched upon some of the aspects that seemed to be arising as a result of the Boeing 737 MAX 8 aspects that have been in the news recently.

My goal was not to figure out the deadly incidents. My intent and hope were that we could glean some useful points and cast those into the burgeoning field of AI self-driving cars. Given how immature the field of AI self-driving car is today in comparison to the maturity of the aircraft industry, there's a lot to be learned and reapplied.

Let's keep things safe out there.

CHAPTER 6

CAR CONTROLS COMMANDS AND AI SELF-DRIVING CAR

CHAPTER 6
CAR CONTROLS COMMANDS AND AI SELF-DRIVING CAR

Which is better, a lead foot on the brakes and a light-foot on the gas, or a lead foot on the gas and a featherweight foot on the brakes? Hard to say. If you are trying to drive onto the freeway, you usually need to double down on the gas pedal and make sure you enter into traffic at a fast and equitable speed. If you are driving in a busy mall parking lot, probably best to keep your foot leaning on the brakes so that you don't hit anyone.

I remember when I was guiding my children on how to drive a car that it seemed like they would inevitably drift toward having a heavy foot and a light foot on each of the respective pedals. Over time, they became proficient in judging how much pressure to apply for the gas and the brakes, doing so as based on the situation and the nature of the driving circumstances involved. Today, they put little conscious thought into the matter and are seasoned drivers.

Novice drivers though aren't quite sure how to treat the car controls. Besides my own children, I've seen the teenagers of other parents that were also apt to misjudge the controls when first learning to drive.

It was somewhat comical one day to watch as a teenager drove down our street and his car seemed to start and stop. One moment the accelerator was being pushed, the next moment the teenager plied on the brakes. This makes sense in that he was concerned once his momentum got going that he was perhaps barreling too fast, so he wanted to slow down, but once he slowed down it became apparent that he needed to add some gas to get going again.

I'm sure we've all had the same experience when trying to learn to drive. I'd also bet that sometimes you've found yourself thrown a kilter when trying to drive someone else's car, and you were unsure of how sensitive the car controls were.

Whenever I rent a car, which I do a lot of the time due to my work travel, I often discover that during the first few minutes of driving the rental car that I am over-controlling it. I need to initially get used to how the brakes react, how the accelerator reacts, and how the steering reacts. It doesn't take long. It does though give you a pause for thought and perhaps allow you to reminisce about the old days of when you first learned to drive.

You might be so familiar with driving your car that it seems nearly unfathomable to imagine that anyone could drive it in a stuttered kind of way. For you, the reaction of the pedals and the steering is now considered "natural" and flows with an ease that you don't likely think about. If someone else tries to drive your car and they have troubles doing so, perhaps mentioning that the pedals are slow to react or overly fast to react, the odds are that you'd be surprised at this response. For you, the pedals and steering are "just right" and have reached a vaunted Goldilocks stage, namely not too easy and not too hard to use.

In referring to the car controls, it is simplest to focus on the brakes, the accelerator, and the steering wheel. Those of course aren't the only car controls you deal with. You need to start the car. You need to put the car into gear, perhaps using reverse to back out of your garage, and then place the car into drive to head down the street that you live on.

Besides the gears, you might have also been using your parking brake. I swear that at least once per month or so that I somehow forget that I had used the parking brake and then upon backing out of my garage, and realizing the car is moving really sluggishly, I sheepishly realize I had forgotten to release the parking brake. Hope it's not a sign of dementia setting in.

You could suggest that your turn indicators or blinkers are also part of your car controls. They don't likely cause the car to do anything in terms of its motion, but they are an important means of informing other drivers and pedestrians about what way you are going to go. I'm guessing you also long ago learned the arm signals that you can also use, placing your arm out the driver's side window to use it as a turn indicator. It is a rarity to do so today.

When I see someone use their arm in this manner, I often do a little laugh at the charm of using such archaic ways (also, does this mean their blinkers are broken, or are they just trying to be a friendly driver, or what is the story?).

Would you say that your headlamps are part of your car controls? It seems a bit of a stretch. You could though argue that they are important to being able to see the road ahead, especially at nighttime. They also can forewarn other drivers of your presence. The headlamps and the fog lamps can be an important element of driving. We can nonetheless debate whether you consider them as a car control or not, since the headlamps don't directly control the movement of the car.

I'm going to herein concentrate on the brakes, the accelerator, and the steering, claiming that those are the core controls of the car. I've mentioned the other control related aspects to make sure that no one accuses me of having forgotten about those other means of controlling the car. Yes, the parking brake can be quite important. Yes, choosing the gear for the car is quite important. And so on. Please just assume that I acknowledge and appreciate their role in the driving task.

Speaking of the parking brake, I learned a handy trick from a college buddy during my wild driving days as a college student.

One day, he was driving his car and I was sitting in the front passenger seat. We were rocketing along and headed from Los Angeles up to the Bay Area, going to a college football game up there. Admittedly, he was going faster than the speed limit. Wrong of us. You have to though realize that there is a lengthy freeway, designated as the 5 freeway, requiring about a 6- or 7-hour drive to get up to the Bay Area from Southern California, and I dare say that everyone driving this highway goes over the speed limit (well, okay, maybe not the truck drivers). You can cut down the drive to around 5 hours if you are willing to inch above the posted speed limit (probably more than just an inch!).

All of a sudden, my friend reached for the parking brake and began to make use of it. This didn't make any sense to me. A parking brake was intended for use when you are parked, or so I had thought. Why in the world was he toying with the parking brake? Had he lost his mind? Did he have some beers before we headed-out, doing a bit of pregaming before we reached our destination? I hoped not.

Upon seeing my quizzical look, he explained that there was a California Highway Patrol (CHP) police car that had gotten onto the freeway and was now behind us, about a quarter mile or so. We were going over the speed limit and a handy target for the CHP to pull us over. My buddy told me that if he used the actual brakes, the brake lights would illuminate. This would be a sure sign that he was trying to bleed off speed and it might spark the CHP to come and give him a speeding ticket.

By using the parking brake, he was able to gradually reduce the speed of the car. This also did not provide any kind of overt clue of what was taking place. Clever? Or, a misguided use of a crucial feature of the car? You decide. In any case, we ended-up going the actual speed limit for much of the rest of the trip, doing so as long as the CHP officer was behind us.

So, as I say, the parking brake is indeed a car control. Likewise, the use of the gears. You likely use the gears in a perfunctory way. Put the car into reverse to back out of your garage, put it into forward or drive to move ahead. You do this similarly when parking in a parking lot. Most of the time, there's not much else involved in dealing with gears, at least in an automated transmission equipped car.

During a camping trip with my son's Boy Scout troop, we drove up into the mountains, and I suddenly became more aware of the gears in my car. On some of the steep roads, I had to put the car into a lower gear. Also, while driving along the winding roads that dipped and rose, I could sense the car doing a lot of shifting among the gears. Usually, the shifting was done without any noticeable indication. On these tougher roads, the shifting became more obvious, both the sounds of the gears shifting and the engine noise, along with the feeling of the car as each gear shift took place.

A good driver is aware of the full gamut of ways in which they can control their car. No tool or feature or driving control should be ignored or forgotten and left to being unused if it can be put to appropriate use (and sometimes inappropriate use, I suppose, such as the parking brake to save us from a speeding ticket).

Focusing on just the brakes, the accelerator, and the steering wheel, let's consider how you make use of those driving controls.

At a tactical level, it's apparent that you use the brakes to slow down the car. You use the accelerator to speed-up the car. You use the steering wheel to redirect the direction of the car. Novice drivers aren't at first sure of which pedal is the brake and which is the gas. They often get confused about which is which. They are also unsure about whether to use their left foot, their right foot, or maybe both feet to control the pedals.

What's kind of interesting about the history of car controls is the evolution to what we have today. In the United States, for example, we earlier in our history had the driving controls on the right side of the car, rather than the left side. This is surprising to most people here in the U.S.

What, the driving controls were the "wrong" way, some ask? Note, wrong meaning that those with driving controls on the left side tend to think that's the proper placement, while those that have their driving controls on the right side tend to think they have the proper placement.

In any case, we have an estimated several hundred million licensed drivers in the United States. California has the most licensed drivers, coming out to around 27 million or so. I mention these rather large numbers to point out that it is quite amazing that all of those people have learned how to drive a car. In fact, it likely didn't take them very long to learn how to drive a car. Furthermore, they drive a car with relative ease, meaning that they don't routinely struggle to control the car and make it go.

Imagine if driving a car was akin to piloting a plane or a spaceship. Think about how much training everyone would need to have. The odds too are that they would need refresher training from time to time. The complexity of the driving controls would cause us all to struggle when driving a car. It would be a chore to have to drive your car, even for a short trip to the grocery store.

Overall, in a kind of Darwinian process, we have landed upon a set of car controls that seems to work for us all. We have evolved cars to a point that the everyday person can drive a car. Plus, they can drive a car again and again. It's almost as easy as riding a bike. Some might say easier since when riding a bike you need to first learn how to balance the bike.

It has all boiled down to a pedal to make the car stop, a pedal to make the car go, and a wheel that you can twist and turn to steer the car. That's about as basic or fundamental as you can be. We could have instead evolved to a device on the dashboard of the car that does the braking and one that does the acceleration, or maybe have knobs on the steering column to do so. We could have evolved to turn the direction of the car via a knob or other contraption, rather than using a steering wheel.

The beauty of the pedals and the steering wheel are their simplicity. They are easy to learn how to use them. Not only are they easy to use, they are devised to be used in a timely fashion. When you need to suddenly turn the car, you can grasp and twist the steering wheel, doing so almost instinctively, and using your arms and hands in a fluid motion as you do so.

The physical act of controlling the car is crucial. If the steering was cumbersome, imagine how bad things would be when you got into a panic situation. Having only a split second available to steer the car, any kind of added effort involved to physically do so would lead to more deaths and destruction. Humans need to have an ability to quickly make use of the controls. That's why the controls are placed where they are.

You might find of interest that there have been studies done about moving or changing the nature of the driving controls. I've already mentioned some ways that they could be physically repositioned. Some suggest that maybe we should just speak to the car controls, using our voice, and not need to do anything physical with our appendages. As you can guess, this would have both advantages and disadvantages (suppose you lost your voice, suppose you uttered a command inadvertently, etc.).

There are numerous studies about how long it takes to make use of the car controls. Length of time to invoke car controls can be a life-or-death matter.

Contemplate for a moment what happens when you see that a dog is racing across the street in front of your car. You must first see the dog doing this, and thus your eyes need to be watching the road. Your brain has to process the aspect that the dog is possibly going to get hit. Your mind needs to decide what to do, determining whether to steer away, or hit the brakes, or speed-up to go around the dog. Once your mind decides what to do, your body needs to physically take the action required.

Even once you've grabbed the steering wheel or jammed your foot onto the brakes, it will take some additional time for the car to respond. There is not an instantaneous reaction of your invoking the car controls commands and having the car do what you want. When you turn the steering wheel, this is conveyed to the wheels of the car, and those wheels need to physically be turned, all of which takes time. Braking the car is the same kind of time delayed facet, meaning that once you've slammed on the brakes, this needs to be enacted by the tires and the braking system, along with the time involved in the physics of the car coming to a halt.

In our minds, we often blur the distinction between acting upon the car controls and the action of the car complying with those controlling actions. Only when you are in a dire situation do you at times become aware of the difference. Within your mind, you might be thinking that the car can stop on a dime, but by the time you move your body and get your foot to pressure the brake pedal, followed by the brakes being actually applied, followed by the tires being engaged by the brakes, followed by the physics of the road and the tires bringing the car to a halt, it can be much longer than you think.

If you've ever slid into an object that you thought you could brake the car before hitting, you know what I mean by this time delayed reaction aspect.

Another way in which you might have become aware of the indirect aspects of using the car controls and seeing what the car does would be in situations like sliding on a wet rain-soaked road or driving in the snow. You turn the wheels in one direction. The car though decides to slide in another direction. You turn the wheel again, hopeful of trying to get the tires to catch onto the roadway surface. You try to accelerate, but perhaps the wheels just spin without getting traction. And so on.

Have you ever had a moment whereby you did one action with the car controls and regretted it, and so immediately tried to undo the action?

I was sitting at a red light waiting to make a right turn, and decided it was safe to go, so I pressured the accelerator to move ahead. All of a sudden, another car came barreling down the street and came into the lane that I was turning into. I realized that my best bet was to halt my right turn. I quickly shifted my foot from the accelerator pedal to the brake pedal.

Fortunately, I came to a halt and avoided colliding with the barreling car. I wondered though what my car must have thought of my actions. Suppose the car was actually alive, maybe akin to a pet, like your pet dog. You jerk the dog (or car) to move forward, but then you just as quickly jerk the dog (or car) to come to a halt. What kind of messed up owner are you? Can't decide what to do, and cause the dog (or car) to undergo strain and stress, presumably needlessly if you had better planned out your actions.

This brings up another point about the use of the car controls. There are the tactical aspects of activating and using the controls, such as putting your foot onto the pedals and using your hands to turn the steering wheel. You normally though are making use of the controls in a more macroscopic way too, at least hopefully you are doing so.

Suppose you want to drive down the street and make a right turn at the corner. There are a series of tactical car control motions that you would undertake. You accelerate to get the car moving down the street. You steer the car to the right side of the road. If there's a parked car at the curbside, you might slightly steer your car to the left to avoid brushing against the parked car. When you near the corner, you likely are steering the car towards the corner itself, and perhaps applying the brakes to slow down so you can readily make the turn.

You've put together a series of tactical car control commands. They are each of their own merit. Yet, they also are part of a larger perspective on what you are trying to achieve. You are wanting to drive down the street, reach the corner, make the turn, and do this without hitting other cars. Doing so has required a series of back-to-back tactical car control command efforts.

Novice drivers often struggle with this overarching aspect. They are at first overwhelmed by the act of merely using the driving controls. That's why most people will have a novice driver initially practice in an empty parking lot. Let the human become familiar with the itsy bitsy aspects of how to use the controls. Once you've mastered that ability, you can then begin to consider how to dovetail those tactical elements into an overall driving plan.

I know that most of you are likely seasoned drivers and perhaps take for granted how easy it is to not only use the car controls, but also tie them together into a series of efforts to achieve a larger goal such as driving down the street to make a turn. As mentioned before, I think it is a miracle that we have hundreds of millions of people that do this each and every day, and yet we don't have pure chaos and pandemonium. Could you get that many people to do something like balance their checkbooks? Driving a car is much harder, and astoundingly we've gotten everyone to do it reasonably well for most of the time.

What does this have to do with AI self-driving cars?

At the Cybernetic AI Self-Driving Car Institute, we are developing AI software for self-driving cars. An essential aspect of AI self-driving cars is the use of the driving car controls by the AI system. There is more to this than perhaps meets the eye.

Allow me to elaborate.

I'd like to first clarify and introduce the notion that there are varying levels of AI self-driving cars. The topmost level is considered Level 5. A Level 5 self-driving car is one that is being driven by the AI and there is no human driver involved. For the design of Level 5 self-driving cars, the auto makers are even removing the gas pedal, brake pedal, and steering wheel, since those are contraptions used by human drivers. The Level 5 self-driving car is not being driven by a human and nor is there an expectation that a human driver will be present in the self-driving car. It's all on the shoulders of the AI to drive the car.

For self-driving cars less than a Level 5, there must be a human driver present in the car. The human driver is currently considered the responsible party for the acts of the car. The AI and the human driver are co-sharing the driving task. In spite of this co-sharing, the human is supposed to remain fully immersed into the driving task and be ready at all times to perform the driving task. I've repeatedly warned about the dangers of this co-sharing arrangement and predicted it will produce many untoward results.

Let's focus herein on the true Level 5 self-driving car. Much of the comments apply to the less than Level 5 self-driving cars too, but the fully autonomous AI self-driving car will receive the most attention in this discussion.

Here's the usual steps involved in the AI driving task:

- Sensor data collection and interpretation
- Sensor fusion
- Virtual world model updating
- AI action planning
- Car controls command issuance

Another key aspect of AI self-driving cars is that they will be driving on our roadways in the midst of human driven cars too. There are some pundits of AI self-driving cars that continually refer to a utopian world in which there are only AI self-driving cars on the public roads. Currently there are about 250+ million conventional cars in the United States alone, and those cars are not going to magically disappear or become true Level 5 AI self-driving cars overnight.

Indeed, the use of human driven cars will last for many years, likely many decades, and the advent of AI self-driving cars will occur while there are still human driven cars on the roads.

This is a crucial point since this means that the AI of self-driving cars needs to be able to contend with not just other AI self-driving cars, but also contend with human driven cars. It is easy to envision a simplistic and rather unrealistic world in which all AI self-driving cars are politely interacting with each other and being civil about roadway interactions. That's not what is going to be happening for the foreseeable future. AI self-driving cars and human driven cars will need to be able to cope with each other.

Returning to the aspects of the car controls, let's consider how the AI is involved in making use of the car controls.

I'll focus on the use of the car controls by the AI system solely, and not cover much about what happens when the AI and the human are trying to both deal with the car controls.

As mentioned earlier, this co-sharing is especially problematic. Imagine that you were driving a car and another human sat next to you in the front seat, having another set of driving controls, and you both could each drive the car in terms of any of you opting to use any of the pedals and turn the steering wheel as you wished. Mind boggling. The two of you would need to really be on the same wavelength and seek to avoid undermining each other. Consider too what would happen when an emergency arose. That makes any kind of coordinated effort even more arduous.

Shifting though to the use of a true Level 5 AI self-driving car, I'm going to walk you through some of the salient facets of what the AI must do about the car controls and issuing of car control commands.

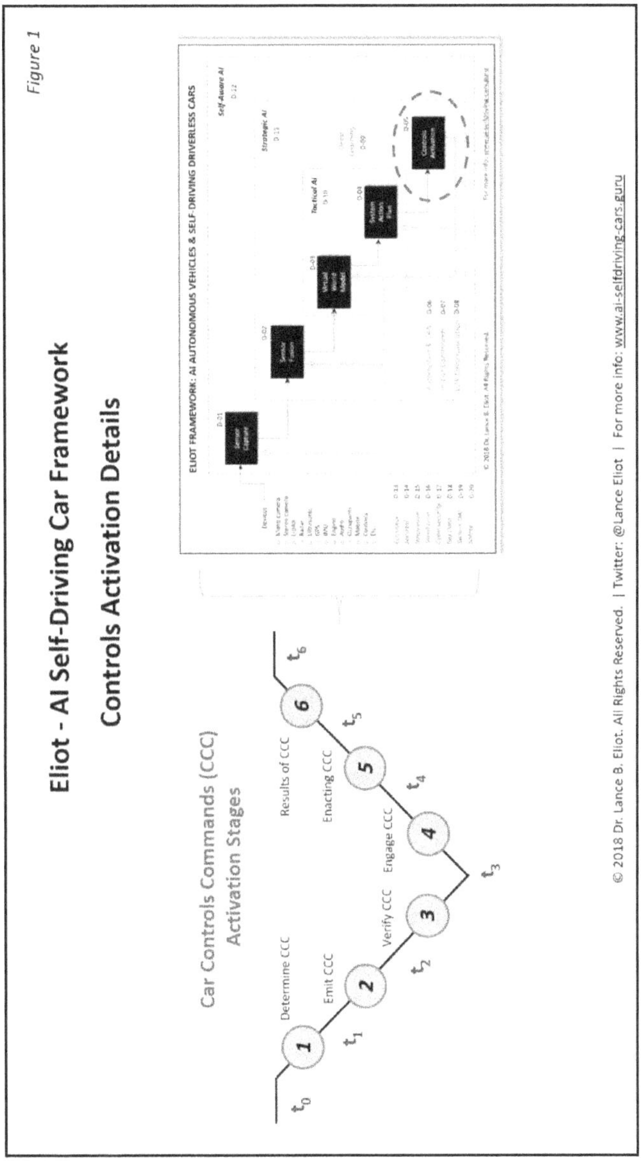
Figure 1
Eliot - AI Self-Driving Car Framework
Controls Activation Details
Car Controls Commands (CCC)
Activation Stages
Determine CCC
Emit CCC
Verify CCC
Engage CCC
Enacting CCC
Results of CCC
ELIOT FRAMEWORK: AI AUTONOMOUS VEHICLES & SELF-DRIVING DRIVERLESS CARS
© 2018 Dr. Lance B. Eliot. All Rights Reserved. | Twitter: @Lance Eliot | For more info: www.ai-selfdriving-cars.guru

Take a look at Figure 1.

There are six major steps involved in generating and enacting of the car controls commands:

1. Determine car control commands to emit
2. Emit car control commands to ECU
3. Verify that car control commands were received and are viable
4. ECU instructs the automotive elements
5. Automotive elements physically enact the received commands
6. Ascertain that car has reacted to the commands

For ease of discussion, we'll assume that there is an ECU (Electronic Control Unit) that translates commands given to it from the AI system and converts those commands into some set of specific operational activities for the car.

The ECU has the task of conveying the operational activities to a myriad of other subsystems that are in the car, including the Brake Control Module (BCM), the Central Timing Module (CTM), the Transmission Control Module (TCM), the Powertrain Control Module (PCM), the Engine Control Module (ECM), etc.

There could easily be one hundred or more such sundry control subsystems that each needs to be properly communicated with and instructed on what needs to be done. You could have all of the protocols and capabilities to do so within the AI system, but this seems unwieldy and generally ill-advised. It makes more sense to hide that detail from the AI system and allow the AI system to be providing commands at a high-level of abstraction.

One important point about this notion of having the AI issues commands at a high-level of abstraction is that you can potentially port the AI system over to other brands and models of cars. If you embed directly into the AI system the specific protocols of a particular model and brand of car, it will likely make it much harder to port the AI system to other cars. By modularizing these aspects and keeping the AI above the fray, you are usually able to more readily port over the AI system.

That being said, let's not kid ourselves. If the AI is far removed from the nature of the underlying car brand and model, it is possible that the AI system won't be able to issue commands that might be feasible for the particular car that the AI is working on. Suppose the AI system emits a car control command that basically asks the car to accelerate from 0 to 60 miles per hour and the AI assumes that this can be done in let's say 3 seconds. That's the speed for sports-oriented cars and it isn't going to work out well for more everyday cars.

Thus, the AI system will likely need to be versed in some aspects of the brand and model car that the AI is running on. Parameters about the specific performance capabilities of the car, and the overall kinds of expected car controls commands, all need to be cooked into the AI action planner that is seeking to ultimately get the self-driving car to do driving actions. It does little good, and actually great potential harm, for the AI system to be expecting the car to perform in ways that the self-driving car is unable or incapable of doing.

Another consideration for the AI system involves the type of network into which the car control commands is going to be conveyed.

Typically, most cars use the Controller Area Network (CAN) vehicle bus as the standard for electronic communications within the car and between the myriad of subsystems. This message-based protocol is both loved and reviled.

First conceived of and released as a formal protocol in the mid-1980s, it has expanded and adapted over the years. There are numerous complimentary protocols that emerged to deal with facets such as device addressing issues, flow control capabilities, and other matters. Weaknesses and qualms often center around CAN's lack of robust security features and difficulties that can ensue when doing troubleshooting of CAN-related problems.

Generally, it is best to try and keep the AI system above the fray about the CAN network, though there needs to be a healthy dose of skepticism built into the AI about what happens once messages are flowing in the CAN and throughout the self-driving car. The AI cannot assume that there will be a perfect conveyance of messages. The AI cannot assume that the conveyance will necessarily happen in as timely a manner as might be otherwise expected. The real-world limitations need to be encompassed by however the AI is going to be expecting the car controls commands to be carried out.

In fact, let's look briefly at each of the six major steps and consider the types of errors or problems that can arise.

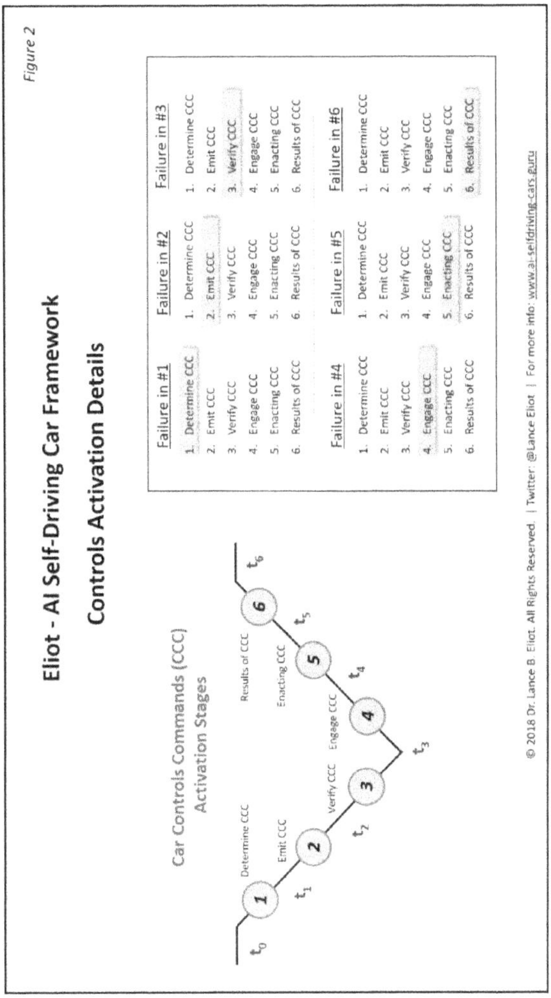
Figure 2
Eliot - AI Self-Driving Car Framework
Controls Activation Details
Car Controls Commands (CCC)
Activation Stages
Determine CCC
Emit CCC
Verify CCC
Engage CCC
Enacting CCC
Results of CCC
Failure in #1
1. Determine CCC
2. Emit CCC
3. Verify CCC
4. Engage CCC
5. Enacting CCC
6. Results of CCC
Failure in #2
1. Determine CCC
2. Emit CCC
3. Verify CCC
4. Engage CCC
5. Enacting CCC
6. Results of CCC
Failure in #3
1. Determine CCC
2. Emit CCC
3. Verify CCC
4. Engage CCC
5. Enacting CCC
6. Results of CCC
Failure in #4
1. Determine CCC
2. Emit CCC
3. Verify CCC
4. Engage CCC
5. Enacting CCC
6. Results of CCC
Failure in #5
1. Determine CCC
2. Emit CCC
3. Verify CCC
4. Engage CCC
5. Enacting CCC
6. Results of CCC
Failure in #6
1. Determine CCC
2. Emit CCC
3. Verify CCC
4. Engage CCC
5. Enacting CCC
6. Results of CCC
© 2018 Dr. Lance B. Eliot. All Rights Reserved. | Twitter: @Lance Eliot | For more info: www.ai-selfdriving-cars.guru

Take a look at Figure 2.

In the first step, determining the car controls commands to emit, it is conceivable that the AI might fail to arrive at a set of car controls commands that it wants to have performed. Perhaps the AI gets gummed up trying to decide what car control commands to use. Maybe the AI hits a snag in the processing, or maybe there's a bug in the system, or maybe the circumstance of the status of the self-driving car has baffled the AI.

Those are obviously bad possibilities. This is why my framework for AI self-driving cars includes the need for the AI to have a self-aware capability that is double checking what the AI system itself is doing. There also needs to be fail-safe features. One of the more intriguing aspects that some are pursuing includes the idea of using AI arguing machines to try and catch these moments when the AI is not seeming to get the job done.

For the second step of emitting the car controls commands, there is a possibility that the commands might be garbled by how they have been formatted or during their conveyance to the ECU. This sets up a rather dangerous situation. If the commands perchance are not intelligible when reaching the ECU, there's a good chance that the ECU will realize something has gone awry, but if the commands are perchance intelligible, the ECU is likely going to try and act on them, though they aren't what was emitted. In essence, the receiving of a wrong set of commands is bound to be worse than commands that are so unintelligible that they are obviously incorrect and improper.

Step three is an effort to checkpoint that the car control commands have indeed been received and an attempt to verify they are what was actually intended. This is a last-moment layer of defense against executing car controls that weren't what was emitted to be undertaken. Note though that this checkpoint is not second-guessing the first two steps, since even if those steps have provided commands that might get the car into an untoward traffic situation, that's not what this third step is trying to ascertain.

In the fourth step, the car controls commands are translated into the myriad of other electronic messages that must be sent along the CAN to the subsystems of the self-driving car. This is when the physical operational activities are being established based on the car controls commands that were provided by step one and step two, and were verified in step three. There are lots of opportunities for things to go south at this juncture. Imagine sending boats along a river with lots of tributaries, and any of those boats might go astray.

During step five, the operational activities are now being carried out, such as the brakes being applied to the tires and the car beginning to slow down or the accelerated applied and the car starting to speed-up. Assuming that the car controls commands actually reached the subsystems in step four, this step five is the actual enactment of those commands. Things can go wrong. Suppose the brakes aren't working right? Suppose the engine is not responsive?

At step six, there is a need to ascertain that the car controls commands were carried out. As a human driver, when you wrench the steering wheel to a hard right, you can feel as the car makes the right lurching motion. This is your way of ascertaining that your command, the steering wheel movement, got translated into the actual operational and physical outcome. The AI system has to do the same kind of sensing to realize whether or not the car controls commands were executed, which requires using the sensors such as the cameras, radar, LIDAR, and internally focused ones like the IMU.

Each of the six major steps takes time to undertake.

The AI system during the action planning portion has to gauge how long each of those steps might take and use that estimation to determine what is feasible to do. If the amount of time to apply the brakes, let's say, would exceed what the AI wants to do in terms of the necessity of trying to slow down or halt the self-driving car, the AI would need to ascertain what another alternative might be pursued instead. For example, if the braking cannot be done in time, would it be possible to turn the steering wheel in time, and avoid whatever collision is about to occur?

As might be rather evident, the AI system cannot just emit car controls commands and walk away from the effort. The AI has to ascertain whether or not the car controls commands were properly and appropriately disseminated and performed. This includes not just that the commands themselves were abided by, but it also includes that the timing of the effort went as planned too. The AI has to be ready to deal with contingencies in case the commands are improperly conveyed, or improperly executed, or executed on a delayed basis, etc.

As a human driver, you likely sometimes change your mind while driving the car and suddenly do something contrary to what you had just done, such as my earlier example of radically going from speeding up to suddenly slowing down. Can the AI "change its mind" in terms of opting to do something different than what it has already started to undertake?

The answer is yes, the AI can opt to try and change what it was trying to do. This can be problematic to execute.

If the AI can catch the emitted commands before the ECU starts to push them along to the self-driving car subsystems, those commands can be potentially suppressed. That's a kind of undo. If the commands are already in-flight of being performed by the physical elements of the self-driving car, there's not much chance of an undo, and instead the AI would likely need to emit a new set of car controls commands, seeking to get those executed right away (such as doing a braking on top of having just done a speeding up action).

Suppose the AI emits commands to turn the steering wheel so radically that it would cause the self-driving car to topple over and roll onto its roof. What step should catch that aspect? Even if it is caught, does the act itself mean that it should never be executed? Perhaps the AI has ascertained that making such a radical turn is worth the risk, namely that it is "better" to turn and roll over the self-driving car versus say ramming into a truck that's filled with petrol and would explode upon impact.

There are also car control commands that could be emitted that are not possible for the physical capabilities of the car. Remember that I earlier mentioned about the notion of going from 0 to 60 miles per hour in 3 seconds. If the AI system emits commands that are based on that capability, and yet if the self-driving car cannot achieve that kind of pace, this is a dangerous disconnect or confusion. One place to have a final double-check is at step 3 of the six major steps.

It would be better though that such commands never get into the stream and the AI should not be relying on a slim chance hope that infeasible or impossible commands are going to get detected and rejects downstream.

Most of these steps are complex and complicated when you get into their respective details. They involve doing a variety of real-time programming and are not particularly AI-based in terms of how you would develop these portions of the overall self-driving car systems. They are more akin to traditional automotive engineering and systems development.

You might be wondering whether AI could help out in those seemingly non-AI related portions. Yes, there are some ways that we can apply AI to those elements.

One aspect involves using Machine Learning or Deep Learning to ferret out patterns of car controls commands actions. If there are patterns that can be found, it could make things easier for the AI system and the controlling of the self-driving car.

We've taken large datasets of emitting car controls commands and fed them into large-scale multi-layer artificial neural networks. This is a means to seek out patterns. There are other ways to do so too, including using other popular techniques. You often would be wise to use an ensemble of Deep Learning techniques. Doing so allows for a wide array of hopefully identifying useful patterns.

To explain why patterns of car controls commands might be handy, consider what you do as a human driver of a car. Let's say that each morning you back your car out of your garage, doing so in reverse, going slowly, and enter into the street while backing out. Once you get far enough into the street, you turn the wheel toward the end of the street and begin to accelerate. You accelerate somewhat toward the end of the block, and then usually make a right turn. All of this is a series of maneuvers that you do each morning, almost like clockwork.

In fact, the odds are that you do this driving sequence somewhat mindlessly. You are perhaps thinking about work and other matters, rather than concentrating on the driving task. You've done the sequence so much that it is rote or muscle memory, nearly acting without any awareness you are doing so. I admit that I do the same. There are some mornings that I reach the end of the block and suddenly am startled, amazed that I did that whole backing out and driving forward sequence, yet my mind was drifting to other topics.

Let's put AI into the driver's seat. Under the usual circumstances, the AI would need to calculate each of those particular actions and figure out what to do. From a raw and unprocessed blank slate, the AI would determine that the self-driving car needs to back out of the garage. Those car control commands would be baked fresh to do so. The AI would determine the self-driving car needs to make its way down the street. Those car control commands would be baked fresh. And so on.

Suppose though that the AI self-driving car had used Machine Learning or Deep Learning to examine the voluminous amount of driving actions of the self-driving car over time. This pattern of each morning doing the same driving routine has a chance of being spotted by the Machine Learning or Deep Learning. If those kinds of driving patterns are identifiable, the AI could incorporate those sets or subsets into a collection or library of known driving patterns. These patterns could then be invoked when needed.

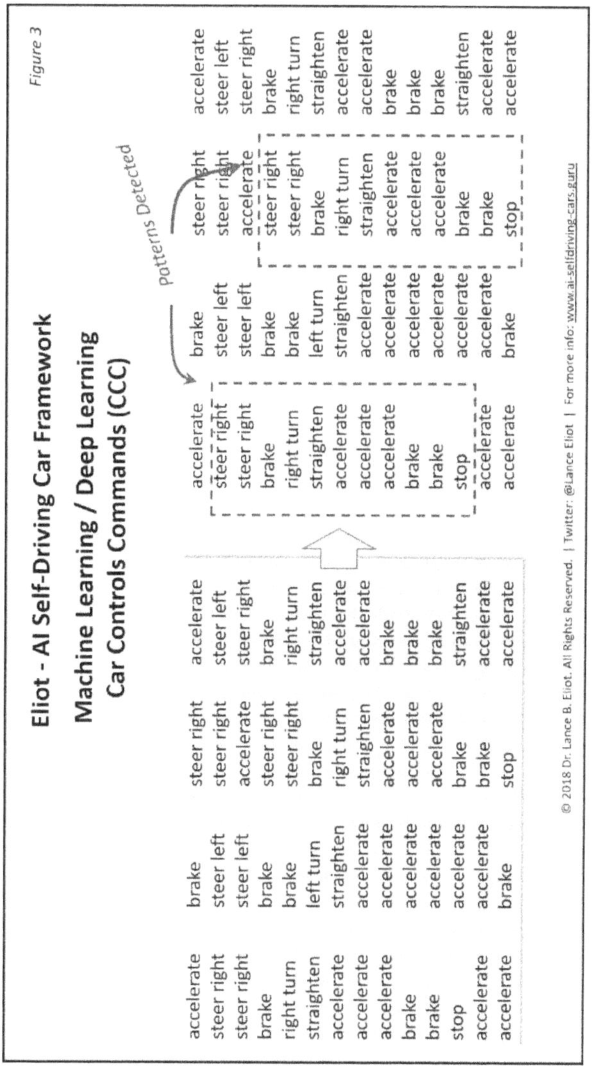
Figure 3
Eliot - AI Self-Driving Car Framework
Machine Learning / Deep Learning
Car Controls Commands (CCC)
accelerate steer right steer right brake right turn straighten accelerate accelerate accelerate brake brake stop accelerate accelerate
brake steer left steer left brake brake left turn straighten accelerate accelerate accelerate accelerate accelerate accelerate brake
steer right steer right accelerate steer right steer right brake right turn straighten accelerate accelerate accelerate brake brake stop
accelerate steer left steer right brake right turn straighten accelerate accelerate brake brake brake straighten accelerate accelerate
Patterns Detected
accelerate steer right steer right brake right turn straighten accelerate accelerate accelerate brake brake stop accelerate accelerate
brake steer left steer left brake brake left turn straighten accelerate accelerate accelerate accelerate accelerate accelerate brake
steer right steer right accelerate steer right steer right brake right turn straighten accelerate accelerate accelerate brake brake stop
accelerate steer left steer right brake right turn straighten accelerate accelerate brake brake brake straighten accelerate accelerate
© 2018 Dr. Lance B. Eliot. All Rights Reserved. | Twitter: @Lance Eliot | For more info: www.ai-selfdriving-cars.guru

Take a look at Figure 3.

Does the invoking of these driving patterns imply that the AI can somehow fall asleep and merely allow those sets to be carried out? Nope. In the same manner that a human driver cannot (should not) blindly perform the same driving pattern, nor can the AI do so.

When I mentioned that I sometimes reach the corner of my street and realize that I was in a kind of mental fog, don't misinterpret that suggestion to mean that I wasn't paying attention to the driving task at all. One day, I started to back out of my garage, and my neighbor's cat was sauntering in the street where I was backing out the car. Had I done my usual backing out, mindlessly, and if the cat had not realized the car was coming (perhaps it had not yet had its morning coffee!), it could have been a murky morning for that cat.

An astute human driver will be paying attention to the driving task even if the driving task is a repetitive one that has become part of their habits of driving. I'm not saying all humans will be quite so diligent and that's part of the problem with human drivers. In any case, the AI would need to still stay on top of its game, doing so while performing a set of car controls commands. At any moment, the sequence might need to be interrupted or altered, depending upon the driving situation at-hand.

Conclusion

Car controls commands are essential to the operation of a self-driving car. They don't get the kind of media attention that you see going toward the sensor's aspects of self-driving cars. Nonetheless, if the AI system and the car controls commands portion aren't properly aligned, it can be a dangerous and very untoward situation.

Though the car control commands aspects are primarily automotive engineering based, there are opportunities to add AI into the mix. One approach involves examining large datasets of car controls commands emissions and trying to find useful patterns. Caution needs to be exercised in doing so. There could be patterns that are not viable for reuse or that are only reusable in quite narrow circumstances.

As a human driver, you are continually issuing car controls commands. They are coming from your brain, going to your limbs, and then involve using the pedals and the steering wheel. The use of the pedals and the steering wheel are then translated into the use of the car subsystems. Once those car subsystems undertake their efforts, the car physically attempts to perform those driving efforts. It's all a dance of the human driver and the car. The same kind of dance has to happen with the AI and the self-driving car.

CHAPTER 7
MULTI-SENSOR DATA FUSION AND AI SELF-DRIVING CARS

CHAPTER 7

MULTI-SENSOR DATA FUSION AND AI SELF-DRIVING CARS

A crucial element of AI self-driving cars is the capability to undertake Multi-Sensor Data Fusion (MSDF), consisting of collecting together and trying to reconcile, harmonize, integrate, and synthesize the data about the surroundings and environment in which the self-driving car is operating. Simple stated, the sensors of the self-driving car are the eyes, ears, and sensory input, while the AI must somehow interpret and assemble the sensory data into a cohesive and usable interpretation of the real world.

If the sensor fusion does a poor job of discerning what's out there, the AI is essentially blind or misled toward making life-or-death algorithmic decisions. Furthermore, the sensor fusion needs to be performed on a timely basis. Any extra time taken to undertake the sensor fusion means there is less time for the AI action planning subsystem to comprehend the driving situation and figure out what driving actions are next needed.

Humans do sensor fusion all the time, in our heads, though we often do not overtly put explicit thought towards our doing so.

It just happens, naturally. We do the sensor fusing by a kind of autonomic process, ingrained by our innate and learned abilities of fusing our sensory inputs from the time we are born. On some occasions, we might be sparked to think about our sensor fusing capacities, if the circumstance catches our attention.

The other day, I was driving in the downtown Los Angeles area. There is always an abundance of traffic, including cars, bikes, motorcycles, scooters, and pedestrians that are prone to jaywalking. There is a lot to pay attention to. Is that bicyclist going to stay in the bike lane or decide to veer into the street? Will the pedestrian eyeing my car decide to leap into the road and dart across the street, making them a target and causing me to hit the brakes? It is a free-for-all.

I had my radio on, listening to the news reports, when I began to faintly hear the sound of a siren, seemingly off in the distance. Maybe it was outside, or maybe it was inside the car -- the siren might actually be part of a radio segment covering the news of a local car accident that had happened that morning on the freeway, or was it instead a siren somewhere outside of my car? I turned down my radio. I quickly rolled down my driver's side window.

As I strained to try and hear a siren, I also kept my eyes peeled, anticipating that if the siren was occurring nearby, there might be a police car or ambulance or fire truck that might soon go skyrocketing past me. These days it seems like most driver's don't care about emergency vehicles and fail to pull over to give them room to zoom along. I'm one of those motorists that still thinks we ought to help out by getting out of the way of the responders (plus, it's the law in California, as it is in most states).

Of course, it makes driving sense anyway to get out of the way, since otherwise you are begging to get into a collision with a fast-moving vehicle, which doesn't seem like a good idea on anyone's behalf.

A few years ago, I saw the aftermath of a collision between a passenger car and an ambulance. The two struck each other with tremendous force. The ambulance ended-up on its side. I happened to drive down the street where the accident had occurred, and the recovery crews were mopping up the scene. It looked outright frightening.

In any case, I was listening intently in the case of my driving in downtown Los Angeles and trying to discern if an emergency vehicle was in my vicinity and warning to be on the watch for it. I could just barely hear the siren. My guess was that it had to be a few blocks away from me. Was it thought getting louder and getting nearer to me, or was it fading and getting further away?

I decided that the siren was definitely getting more distinctive and pronounced. The echoes along the streets and buildings was creating some difficulty in deciding where the siren was coming from. I could not determine if the siren was behind me or somewhere in front of me. I couldn't even tell if the siren was to my left or to my right. All I could seem to guess is that it was getting closer, one way or another.

At times like this, your need to do some sensor fusion is crucial. Your eyes are looking for any telltale sign of an emergency vehicle. Maybe the flashing lights might be seen from a distance. Perhaps other traffic might start to make way for the emergency vehicle, and that's a visual clue that the vehicle is coming from a particular direction. Your ears are being used to do a bat-like echolocation of the emergency vehicle, using the sound to gauge the direction, speed, and placement of the speeding object.

I became quite aware of my having to merge together the sounds of the siren with my visual search of the traffic and streets. Each was feeding the other. I could see traffic up ahead that was coming to a stop, doing so even though they had a green light. It caused me to roll down my other window, the front passenger side window, in hopes of aiding my detection of the siren.

Sure enough, the sound of the siren came through quite a bit on the right side of my car, more so than the left side of the car. I turned my head toward the right, and in moments saw the ambulance that zipped out of a cross-street and came into the lanes ahead.

This is the crux of Multi-Sensor Data Fusion. I had one kind of sensor, my eyes, providing visual inputs to my brain. I had another kind of sensor, my ears, providing acoustical inputs to my brain. My brain managed to tie together the two kinds of inputs. Not only were the inputs brought together, they were used in a means of each aiding the other. My visual processing led me to listen toward the sound. The sound led me to look toward where the sound seemed to be coming from.

My mind, doing some action planning of how to drive the car, melded together the visual and the acoustic, using it to guide how I would drive the car. In this case, I pulled the car over and came to a near stop. I also continued to listen to the siren. Only once it had gone far enough away, along with my not being able to see the emergency vehicle anymore, did I decide to resume driving down the street.

This whole activity of my doing the sensor fusion was something that played out in just a handful of seconds. I know that my describing it seemed to suggest that it took a long time to occur, but the reality is that the whole thing happened like this, hear siren, try to find siren, match siren with what I see, pull over, wait, and then resume driving once safe to do so. It is a pretty quick effort. You likely do the same from time-to-time.

Suppose though that I was wearing my ear buds and listening to loud music while driving (not a wise thing to do when driving a car, and usually illegal to do while driving), and did not hear the siren? I would have been solely dependent upon my sense of sight. Usually, it is better to have multiple sensors active and available when driving a car, giving you a more enriched texture of the traffic and the driving situation.

Notice too that the siren was hard to pin down in terms of where it was coming from, along with how far away it was. This highlights the aspect that the sensory data being collected might be only partially received or might otherwise be scant, or even faulty. Same could be said about my visually trying to spot the emergency vehicle. The tall buildings blocked my overall view. The other traffic tended to also block my view. If it had been raining, my vision would have been further disrupted.

Another aspect involves attempting to square together the inputs from multiple sensors. Imagine if the siren was getting louder and louder, and yet I did not see any impact to the traffic situation, meaning that no other cars changed their behavior and those pedestrians kept jaywalking. That would have been confusing. The sounds and my ears would seem to be suggesting one thing, while my eyes and visual processing was suggesting something else. It can be hard at times to mentally resolve such matters.

In this case, I was alone in my car. Only me and my own "sensors" were involved in this multi-sensor data fusion. You could have more such sensors, such as when having passengers that can aid you in the driving task.

I recall during my college days a rather harried driving occasion. While driving to a college basketball game, I managed to get into a thick bank of fog. Some of my buddies were in the car with me. At first, I was tempted to pull the car over and wait out the fog, hoping it would dissipate. My friends in the car were eager to get to the game and urged me to keep driving. I pointed out that I could barely see in front of the car and had zero visibility of anything behind the car.

Not the best way to be driving at highway speeds on an open highway. Plus, it was night time. A potent combination for a car wreck. It wasn't just me that I was worried about, I also was concerned for my friends.

And, even though I thought I could drive through the fog, those other idiot drivers that do so without paying close attention to the road were the really worrisome element. All it would take is some dolt to ram into me or opt to suddenly jam on their brakes, and it could be a bad evening for us all.

Here's what happened. My buddy in the front passenger seat offered to intently watch for anything to my right. The two friends in the back seat were able to turnaround and look out the back window. I suddenly had the power of six additional eyeballs, all looking for any other traffic. They began each verbally reporting their respective status. I don't see anything, one said. Another one barked out that a car was coming from my right and heading toward us. I turned my head and swerved the car to avoid what might have been a collision.

Meanwhile, both of the friends in the backseat yelled out that a car was rapidly approaching toward the rear of the car. They surmised that the driver had not seen our car in the fog and was going to run right up into us. I hit the gas to accelerate forward, doing so to gain a distance gap between me and the car from behind. I could see that there wasn't a car directly ahead of me and so leaping forward was a reasonable gambit to avoid getting hit from behind.

All in all, we made it to the basketball game without nary a nick. It was a bit alarming though and a situation that I will always remember. There we were, working as a team, with me as the driver at the wheel. I had to do some real sensor fusion. I was receiving data from my own eyes, along with hearing from my buddies, and having to mentally combine together what they were telling me with what I could actually see.

When you are driving a car, you often are doing Multi-Target Tracking (MTT). This involves identifying particular objects or "targets" that you are trying to keep an eye on. While driving in downtown Los Angeles, my "targets" included the many cars, bike rides, and pedestrians. While driving in the foggy evening, we had cars coming from the right and from behind.

Your Field of View (FOV) is another vital aspect of driving a car and using your sensory apparatus. During the fog, my own FOV was narrowed to what I could see on the driver's side of the car, and I could not see anything from behind the car. Fortunately, my buddies provided additional FOV's. My front passenger was able to augment my FOV by telling me what was seen to the right of the car. The two in the backseat had a FOV of what was behind the car.

Those two stories that I've told are indicative of how we humans do our sensor fusion while driving a car. As I earlier mentioned, we often don't seemingly put any conscious thought to the matter. By watching a teenage novice driver, you can at times observe as they struggle to do sensor fusion. They are new to driving and trying to cope with the myriad of details to be handled. It is a lot to process, such as keeping your hands on the wheel, your feet on the pedals, your eyes on the road, along with having to mentally process everything that is happening, all at once, in real-time.

It can be overwhelming. Seasoned drivers are used to it. But seasoned drivers can also find themselves in situations whereby sensor fusion becomes an outright imperative and involves very deliberate attention and thought. My fog story is somewhat akin to that kind of situation, similarly my siren listening story is another example.

In the news recently there has been the story about the Boeing 737 MAX 8 airplane and in particular two horrific deadly crashes. Some believe that the sensors on the plane were a significant contributing factor to the crashes. Though the matters are still being investigated, it is a potential example of the importance of Multi-Sensor Data Fusion and has lessons that can be applied to driving a car and advanced automation used to do so.

Multi-Sensor Data Fusion for AI Self-Driving Cars

What does this have to do with AI self-driving cars?

At the Cybernetic AI Self-Driving Car Institute, we are developing AI software for self-driving cars. One important aspect involves the design, development, testing, and fielding of the Multi-Sensor Data Fusion.

Allow me to elaborate.

I'd like to first clarify and introduce the notion that there are varying levels of AI self-driving cars. The topmost level is considered Level 5. A Level 5 self-driving car is one that is being driven by the AI and there is no human driver involved. For the design of Level 5 self-driving cars, the auto makers are even removing the gas pedal, brake pedal, and steering wheel, since those are contraptions used by human drivers. The Level 5 self-driving car is not being driven by a human and nor is there an expectation that a human driver will be present in the self-driving car. It's all on the shoulders of the AI to drive the car.

For self-driving cars less than a Level 5, there must be a human driver present in the car. The human driver is currently considered the responsible party for the acts of the car. The AI and the human driver are co-sharing the driving task. In spite of this co-sharing, the human is supposed to remain fully immersed into the driving task and be ready at all times to perform the driving task. I've repeatedly warned about the dangers of this co-sharing arrangement and predicted it will produce many untoward results.

Let's focus herein on the true Level 5 self-driving car. Much of the comments apply to the less than Level 5 self-driving cars too, but the fully autonomous AI self-driving car will receive the most attention in this discussion.

Here's the usual steps involved in the AI driving task:

- Sensor data collection and interpretation
- Sensor fusion
- Virtual world model updating
- AI action planning
- Car controls command issuance

Another key aspect of AI self-driving cars is that they will be driving on our roadways in the midst of human driven cars too. There are some pundits of AI self-driving cars that continually refer to a utopian world in which there are only AI self-driving cars on the public roads. Currently there are about 250+ million conventional cars in the United States alone, and those cars are not going to magically disappear or become true Level 5 AI self-driving cars overnight.

Indeed, the use of human driven cars will last for many years, likely many decades, and the advent of AI self-driving cars will occur while there are still human driven cars on the roads. This is a crucial point since this means that the AI of self-driving cars needs to be able to contend with not just other AI self-driving cars, but also contend with human driven cars. It is easy to envision a simplistic and rather unrealistic world in which all AI self-driving cars are politely interacting with each other and being civil about roadway interactions. That's not what is going to be happening for the foreseeable future. AI self-driving cars and human driven cars will need to be able to cope with each other.

Returning to the topic of Multi-Sensor Data Fusion, let's walk through some of the key essentials of how AI self-driving cars undertake such efforts.

Take a look at Figure 1.

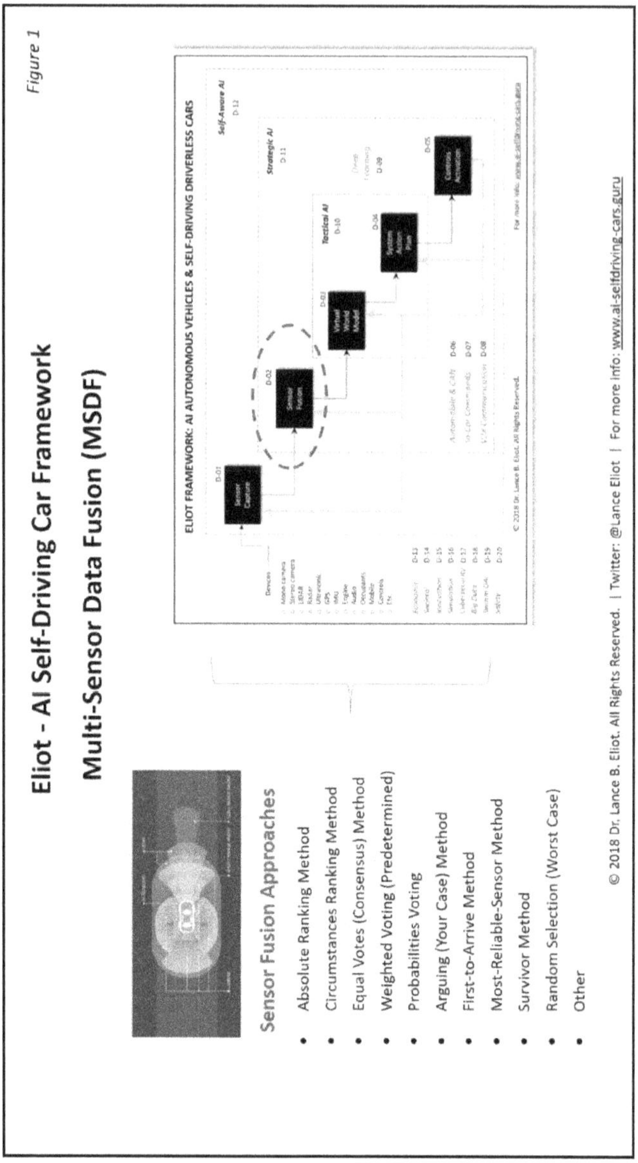
Figure 1
Eliot - AI Self-Driving Car Framework
Multi-Sensor Data Fusion (MSDF)
ELIOT FRAMEWORK: AI AUTONOMOUS VEHICLES & SELF-DRIVING DRIVERLESS CARS
Sensor Capture
Sensor Fusion
Virtual World Model
System Action Plan
Controls Activation
Sensor Fusion Approaches
• Absolute Ranking Method
• Circumstances Ranking Method
• Equal Votes (Consensus) Method
• Weighted Voting (Predetermined)
• Probabilities Voting
• Arguing (Your Case) Method
• First-to-Arrive Method
• Most-Reliable-Sensor Method
• Survivor Method
• Random Selection (Worst Case)
• Other
© 2018 Dr. Lance B. Eliot. All Rights Reserved. | Twitter: @Lance Eliot | For more info: www.ai-selfdriving-cars.guru

I've shown my overall framework about AI self-driving cars and highlighted the sensor fusion stage of processing.

Per my earlier remarks about the crucial nature of sensor fusion, consider that if the sensor fusion goes awry, it means that the stages downstream are going to be either without needed information or be using misleading information. The virtual world model won't be reflective of the real-world surrounding the self-driving car. The AI action planning stage will not be able to make appropriate determinations about what the AI self-driving car actions should be.

One of the major challenges for sensor fusion involves dealing with how to collectively stich together the multitude of sensory data being collected.

You are going to have the visual data collected via the cameras, coming from likely numerous cameras mounted at the front, back, and sides of the self-driving car. There is the radar data collected by the multiple radar sensors mounted on the self-driving car. There are likely ultrasonic sensors. There could be LIDAR sensors, a special kind of sensor that combines light and radar. And there could be other sensors too, such as acoustic sensors, olfactory sensors, etc.

Thus, you will have to stitch together sensor data from like-sensors, such as the data from the various cameras. Plus, you will have to stitch together the sensor data from unlike sensors, meaning that you want to do a kind of comparison and contrasting with the cameras, with the radar, with the LIDAR, with the ultrasonic, and so on.

Each different type or kind of sensor provides a different type or kind of potential indication about the real-world. They do not all perceive the world in the same way. This is both good and bad.

The good aspect is that you can potentially achieve a rounded balance by using differing kinds or types of sensors. Cameras and visual processing are usually not as adept at being indicative of the speed of an object as does the radar or the LIDAR.

By exploiting the strengths of each kind of sensor, you are able to have a more enriched texturing of what the real-world consists of.

If the sensor fusion subsystem is poorly devised, it can undermine this complimentary triangulation that having differing kinds of sensors inherently provides. It's a shame. Weak or slimly designed sensor fusion often tosses away important information that could be used to better gauge the surroundings. With a properly concocted complimentary perspective, the AI action planner portion has a greater shot at making better driving decisions because it is more informed about the real-world around the self-driving car.

Let's though all acknowledge that the more processing you do of the multitude of sensors, the more computer processing you need, which then means that you have to place more computer processors and memory on-board the self-driving car. This adds cost, it adds weight to the car, it consumes electrical power, it generates heat, and has other downsides. Furthermore, trying to bring together all of the data and interpretations is going to take processing time, of which, as emphasized herein many times, the time constraints for the AI are quite severe when driving a car.

Four Key Ways Approaches to MSDF Assimilation

Let's consider the fundamental ways that you assimilate together the sensory data from multiple sensors.

Take a look at Figure 2.

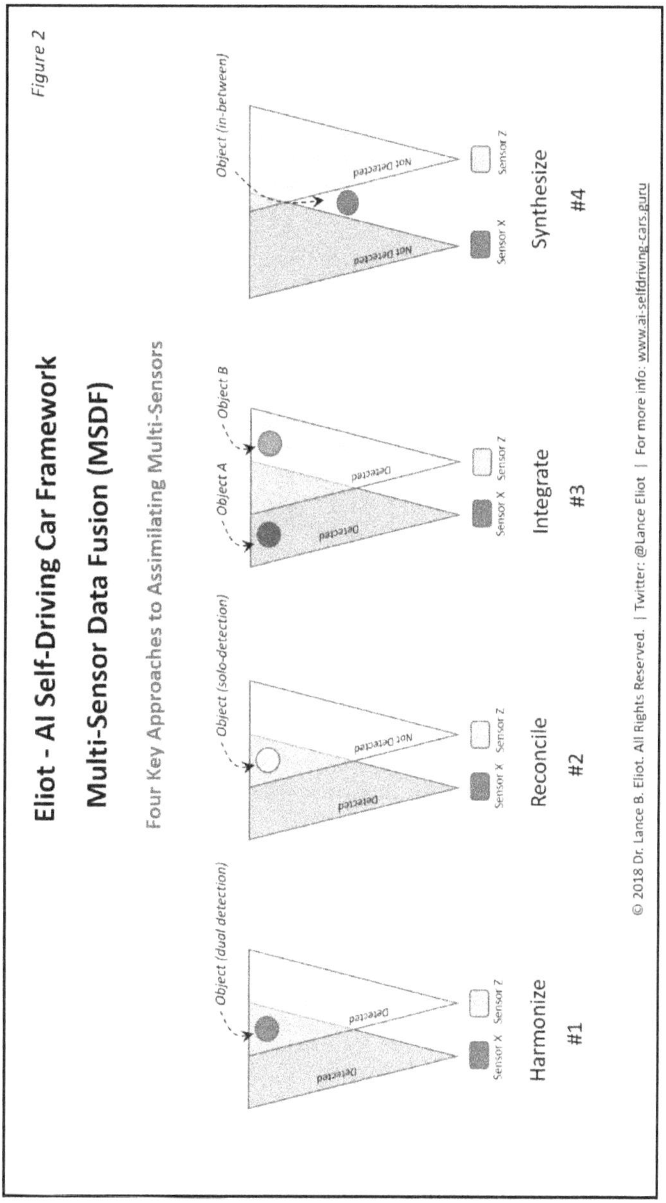
Eliot - AI Self-Driving Car Framework
Multi-Sensor Data Fusion (MSDF)
Four Key Approaches to Assimilating Multi-Sensors
Figure 2
Object (dual detection)
Detected
Detected
Sensor X
Sensor Z
Harmonize
#1
Object (solo-detection)
Detected
Not Detected
Sensor X
Sensor Z
Reconcile
#2
Object A
Object B
Detected
Detected
Sensor X
Sensor Z
Integrate
#3
Object (in-between)
Not Detected
Not Detected
Sensor X
Sensor Z
Synthesize
#4
© 2018 Dr. Lance B. Eliot. All Rights Reserved. | Twitter: @Lance Eliot | For more info: www.ai-selfdriving-cars.guru

I'll briefly describe the four approaches, consisting of harmonize, reconcile, integrate, and synthesize.

- Harmonize

Assume that you have two different kinds of sensors, I'll call them sensor X and sensor Z. They each are able to sense the world outside of the self-driving car. We won't concern ourselves for the moment with their respective strengths and weaknesses, which I'll be covering later on herein.

There is an object in the real-world and the sensor X and the sensor Z are both able to detect the object. This could be a pedestrian in the street, or maybe a dog, or could be a car. In any case, I'm going to simplify the matter to considering the overall notion of detecting an object.

This dual detection means that both of the different kinds of sensors have something to report about the object. We have a dual detection of the object. Now, we want to figure out how much more we can discern about the object because we have two perspectives about it.

This involves harmonizing the two reported detections. Let's pretend that both sensors detect the distance of the object. And, sensor X indicates the object is six feet tall and about two feet wide. Meanwhile, sensor Z is reporting that the object is moving toward the self-driving car, doing so at a speed of a certain number of feet per second N. We can combine together the two sensor reports and update the virtual world model that there is an object of six feet in height, two feet in width, moving toward the self-driving car at some speed N.

Suppose we only relied upon sensor X. Maybe because we only have sensor X and there is no sensor Z on this self-driving car. Or, sensor Z is broken. Or, sensor Z is temporarily out of commission because there is a bunch of mud sitting on top of the sensor.

In this case, we would know only the height and weight and general position of the object, but not have a reading about its speed and direction of travel. That would mean that the AI action planner is not going to have as much a perspective on the object as might be desired.

As a quick aside, this also ties into ongoing debates about which sensors to have on AI self-driving cars. For example, one of the most acrimonious debates involves the choice by Tesla and Elon Musk to not put LIDAR onto the Tesla cars. Elon has stated that he doesn't believe LIDAR is needed to achieve a true AI Level 5 self-driving car via his Autopilot system, though he also acknowledges that he might ultimately be proven mistaken by this assumption.

Some would claim that the sensory input available via LIDAR cannot be otherwise fully devised via the other kinds of sensors, and so in that sense the Tesla's are not going to have the same kind of complimentary or triangulation available that self-driving cars with LIDAR have. Those that are not enamored of LIDAR would claim that the LIDAR sensory data is not worth the added cost, nor worth the added processing effort, nor worth the added cognition time required for processing.

I've pointed out that this is not merely a technical or technological question. It is my bet that once AI self-driving cars get into foul car accidents, we'll see lawsuits that will attempt to go after the auto makers and tech firms for the sensory choices made in the designs of their AI self-driving cars.

If an auto maker or tech firm opted to not use LIDAR, a lawsuit might contend that the omission of LIDAR was a significant drawback to the capabilities of the AI self-driving car, and that the auto maker or tech firm knew or should have known that they were under-powering their AI self-driving car, making it less safe. This is going to be a somewhat "easier" claim to launch, especially due to the aspect that most AI self-driving cars are being equipped with LIDAR.

If an auto maker or tech firm opts to use LIDAR, a lawsuit might contend that the added effort by the AI system to process the LIDAR was a contributor to the car wreck, and that the auto maker or tech firm knew or should have known that the added processing and processing time could lead to the AI self-driving car being less safe. This claim will be more difficult to lodge and support, especially since it goes against the tide of most AI self-driving cars being equipped with LIDAR.

- Reconcile

I'd like to revisit the use of sensor X and sensor Z in terms of object detection.

Let's pretend that sensor X detects an object, and yet sensor Z does not, even though the sensor Z could have. In other words, the object is within the Field of View (FOV) of sensor Z, and yet sensor Z isn't detecting the object. Note that this is vastly different than if the object were entirely outside the FOV of sensor Z, in which case we would not have any expectation that sensor Z could detect the object.

We have a bit of a conundrum on our hands that needs reconciling.

Sensor X says the object is there in the FOV. Sensor Z says the object is not there in the same FOV intersection. Yikes! It could be that sensor X is correct and sensor Z is incorrect. Perhaps sensor Z is faulty, or obscured, or having some other difficulty. On the other hand, maybe sensor X is incorrect, namely that there isn't an object there, and the sensor is X is mistaken, reporting a "ghost" of sorts, something that is not really there, while sensor Z is correct in reporting that there isn't anything there.

There are various means to try and reconcile these seemingly contradictory reports. I'll be getting to those methods shortly herein.

- Integrate

Let's suppose we have two objects. One of those objects is in the FOV of sensor X. The other object is within the FOV of sensor Z. Sensor X is not able to directly detect the object that sensor Z has detected, rightfully so because the object is not inside the FOV of sensor X. Sensor Z is not able to directly detect the object that sensor X has detected, rightfully so because the object is not inside the FOV of sensor Z.

Everything is okay in that the sensor X and sensor Z are both working as expected.

What we would like to do is see if we can integrate together the reporting of sensor X and sensor Z. They each are finding objects in their respective FOV. It could be that the object in the FOV of sensor Z is heading toward the FOV of sensor X, and thus it might be possible to inform sensor X to especially be on the watch for the object. Likewise, the same could be said about the object that sensor X currently has detected and might forewarn sensor Z.

My story about driving in the fog is a similar example of integrating together sensory data. The cars seen by my front passenger and by those sitting in the backseat of my car were integrated into my own mental processing about the driving scene.

- Synthesize

In the fourth kind of approach about assimilating together the sensory data, you can have a situation whereby neither sensor X and nor sensor Z has an object within their respective FOV's. In this case, the assumption would be that neither one even knows that the object exists.

In the case of my driving in the fog, suppose a bike rider was in my blind spot, and that neither of my buddies saw the bike rider due to the fog. None of us knew that a bike rider was nearby. We are all blind to the bike rider. There are likely going to be gaps in the FOV's of the sensors on an AI self-driving car, which suggests that at times there will be parts or objects of the surrounding real-world that the AI action planner is not going to know is even there.

You sometimes have a chance at guessing about objects that aren't in the FOV's of the sensors by interpreting and interpolating whatever you do know about the objects within the FOV's of the sensors. This is referred to as synthesis or synthesizing of sensor fusion.

Remember how I mentioned that I saw other cars moving over when I was hearing the sounds of a siren. I could not see the emergency vehicle. Luckily, I had a clue about the emergency vehicle because I could hear it. Erase the hearing aspects and pretend that all that you had was the visual indication that other cars were moving over to the side of the road.

Within your FOV, you have something happening that gives you a clue about what is not within your FOV. You are able to synthesize what you do know and use that to try and predict what you don't know. It seems like a reasonable guess that if cars around you are pulling over, it suggests an emergency vehicle is coming. I guess it could mean that aliens from Mars have landed and you didn't notice it because you were strictly looking at the other cars, but I doubt that possibility of those alien creatures landing here.

So, you can use the sensory data to try and indirectly figure out what might be happening in FOV's that are outside of your purview. Keeping in mind that this is real-time system and that the self-driving car is in-motion, it could be that within moments the thing that you guessed might be in the outside of scope FOV will come within the scope of your FOV, and hopefully you'll have gotten ready for it. Just as I did about the ambulance that zipped past me.

Voting Methods of Multi-Sensor Data Fusion

When you have multiple sensors and you want to bring together in some cohesive manner their respective reporting, there are a variety of methods you can use.

Take a look at Figure 1 again.

I'll briefly describe each of the voting methods.

- Absolute Ranking Method

In this method, you beforehand decide a ranking of sensors. You might declare that the cameras are higher ranked than the radar. The radar you might decide is higher ranked than the LIDAR. And so on. During sensor fusion, the subsystem uses that predetermined ranking.

For example, suppose you get into a situation of reconciliation, such as the instance I described earlier involving sensor X detecting an object in its FOV but that sensor Z in the intersecting FOV did not detect. If sensor X is the camera, while sensor Z is the LIDAR, you might simply use the pre-determined ranking and the algorithm assumes that since the camera is higher ranking it is "okay" that the sensor Z does not detect the object.

There are tradeoffs to this approach. It tends to be fast, easy to implement, and simple. Yet it tends toward doing the kind of "tossing out" that I forewarned is not usually advantageous overall.

- Circumstances Ranking Method

This is similar to the Absolute Ranking Method but differs because the ranking is changeable depending upon the circumstance in-hand. For example, we might have setup that if there is rainy weather, the camera is no longer the top dog and instead the radar gets the topmost ranking, due to its less likelihood of being adversely impacted by the rain.

There are tradeoffs to this approach too. It tends to be relatively fast, easy to implement, and simple. Yet it once again tends toward doing the kind of "tossing out" that I forewarned is not usually advantageous overall.

- Equal Votes (Consensus) Method

In this approach, you allow each sensor to have a vote. They are all considered equal in their voting capacity. You then use a counting algorithm that might go with a consensus vote. If some threshold of the sensors all agrees about an object, while some do not, you allow the consensus to decide what the AI system is going to be led to believe.

Like the other methods, there are tradeoffs in doing things this way.

- Weighted Voting (Predetermined)

Somewhat similar to the Equal Votes approach, this approach adds a twist and opts to assume that some of the voters are more important than the others. We might have a tendency to believe that the camera is more dependable than the radar, so we give the camera a higher weighted factor. And so on.

Like the other methods, there are tradeoffs in doing things this way.

- Probabilities Voting

You could introduce the use of probabilities into what the sensors are reporting. How certain is the sensor? It might have its own controlling subsystem that can ascertain whether the sensor has gotten bona fide readings or maybe has not been able to do so. The probabilities are then encompassed into the voting method of the multiple sensors.

Like the other methods, there are tradeoffs in doing things this way.

- Arguing (Your Case) Method

A novel approach involves having each of the sensors argue for why their reporting is the appropriate one to use. It's an intriguing notion. We'll have to see whether this can demonstrate sufficient value to warrant being used actively. Research and experimentation are ongoing.

Like the other methods, there are tradeoffs in doing things this way.

- First-to-Arrive Method

This approach involves declaring a kind of winner as to the first sensor that provides its reporting is the one that you'll go with. The advantage is that for timing purposes, you presumably won't wait for the other sensors to report, which then speeds up the sensor fusion effort. On the other hand, you don't know if a split second later one of the other sensors might report something of a contrary nature or that might be an indication of imminent danger that the first sensor did not detect.

Like the other methods, there are tradeoffs in doing things this way.

- Most-Reliable Method

In this approach, you keep track of the reliability of the myriad of sensors on the self-driving car. The sensor that is most reliable will then get the nod when there is a sensor related data dispute.

Like the other methods, there are tradeoffs in doing things this way.

- Survivor Method

It could be that the AI self-driving car is having troubles with the sensors. Maybe the self-driving car is driving in a storm. Several of the sensors might not be doing any viable reporting. Or, perhaps the self-driving car has gotten sideswiped by another car, damaging many of the sensors. This approach involves selecting the sensors based on their survivorship.

Like the other methods, there are tradeoffs in doing things this way.

- Random Selection (Worst Case)

One approach that is obviously controversial involves merely choosing among the sensor fusion choice by random selection, doing so if there seems to not be any other more systemic way to choose between multiple sensors if they are in disagreement about what they have or have not detected.

Like the other methods, there are tradeoffs in doing things this way.

- Other

You can use several of these methods in your sensor fusion subsystem. They can each come to play when the subsystem determines that one approach might be better than the other.

There are other ways that the sensor fusion voting can also be arranged.

How Multiple Sensors Differ is Quite Important

Your hearing is not the same as your vision. When I heard a siren, I was using one of my senses, my ears. They are unlike my eyes. My eyes cannot hear, at least I don't believe they can. This highlights that there are going to be sensors of different kinds.

An overarching goal or structure of the Multi-Sensor Data Fusion involves trying to leverage the strengths of each sensor type, while also minimizing or mitigating the weaknesses of each type of sensor.

One significant characteristic of each type of sensor will be the distance at which it can potentially detect objects. This is one of the many crucial characteristics about sensors.

The further out that the sensor can detect, the more lead time and advantage goes to the AI driving task. Unfortunately, often the further reach also comes with caveats, such as the data at the far ends might be lackluster or suspect. The sensor fusion needs to be established as to the strengths and weaknesses based on the distances involved.

Here's the typical distances for contemporary sensors, though keep in mind that daily improvements are being made in the sensor technology and these numbers are rapidly changing accordingly.

- Main Forward Camera: 150 m (about 492 feet) typically, condition dependent
- Wide Forward Camera: 60 m (about 197 feet) typically, condition dependent
- Narrow Forward Camera: 250 m (about 820 feet) typically, conditions dependent
- Forward Looking Side Camera: 80 m (about 262 feet) typically, condition dependent
- Rear View Camera: 50 m (about 164 feet) typically, condition dependent
- Rearward Looking Side Camera: 100 m (about 328 feet) typically, condition dependent
- Radar: 160 m (about 524 feet) typically, conditions dependent
- Ultrasonic: 8 m (about 26 feet) typically, condition dependent
- LIDAR: 200 m (about 656 feet) typically, condition dependent

There are a number of charts that attempt to depict the strengths and weaknesses when comparing the various sensor types. I suggest you interpret any such chart with a grain of salt. I've seen many such charts that made generalizations that are either untrue or at best misleading.

Also, the number of criteria that can be used to compare sensors is actually quite extensive, and yet the typical comparison chart only picks a few of the criteria. Once again, use caution in interpreting those kinds of short shrift charts.

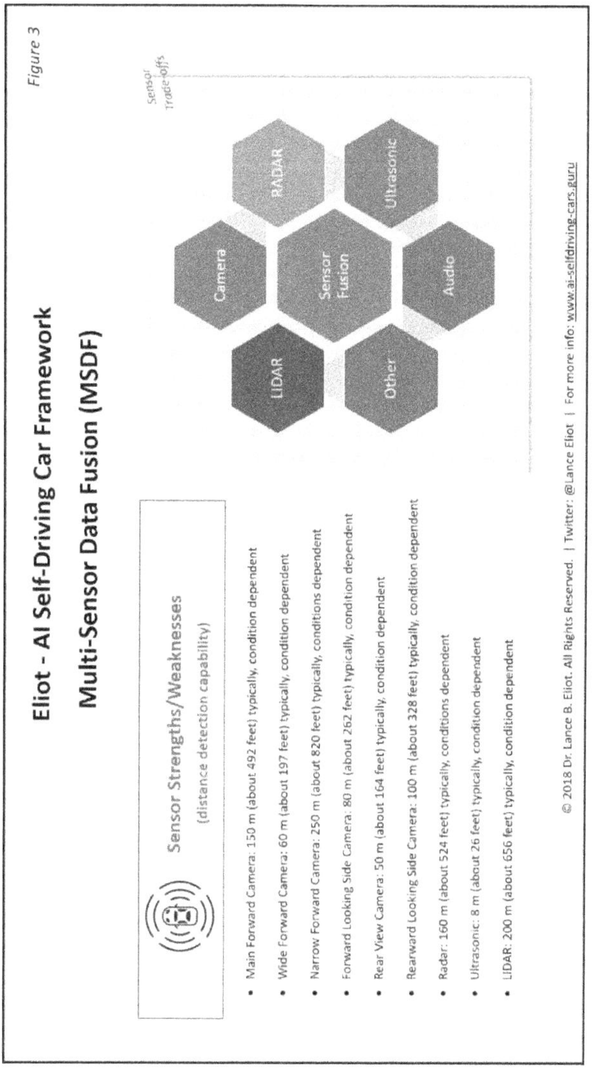
Eliot - AI Self-Driving Car Framework
Multi-Sensor Data Fusion (MSDF)
Figure 3
Sensor Strengths/Weaknesses
(distance detection capability)
• Main Forward Camera: 150 m (about 492 feet) typically, condition dependent
• Wide Forward Camera: 60 m (about 197 feet) typically, condition dependent
• Narrow Forward Camera: 250 m (about 820 feet) typically, conditions dependent
• Forward Looking Side Camera: 80 m (about 262 feet) typically, condition dependent
• Rear View Camera: 50 m (about 164 feet) typically, condition dependent
• Rearward Looking Side Camera: 100 m (about 328 feet) typically, condition dependent
• Radar: 160 m (about 524 feet) typically, conditions dependent
• Ultrasonic: 8 m (about 26 feet) typically, condition dependent
• LIDAR: 200 m (about 656 feet) typically, condition dependent
LIDAR
Camera
RADAR
Sensor Fusion
Other
Audio
Ultrasonic
Sensor Trade-offs
© 2018 Dr. Lance B. Eliot. All Rights Reserved. | Twitter: @Lance Eliot | For more info: www.ai-selfdriving-cars.guru

To give you a bit of an indication about the variety of factors or criteria, here's a handy list to consider:

- Object detection
- Object distinction
- Object classification
- Object shape
- Object edges
- Object speed
- Object direction
- Object granularity
- Maximum Range
- Close-in proximity
- Width of detection
- Speed of detection
- Nighttime impact
- Brightness impact
- Size of sensor
- Placement of sensor
- Cost of sensor
- Reliability of sensor
- Resiliency of sensor
- Snow impact
- Rain impact
- Fog impact
- Software for sensor
- Complexity of use
- Maintainability
- Repairability
- Replaceability
- Etc.

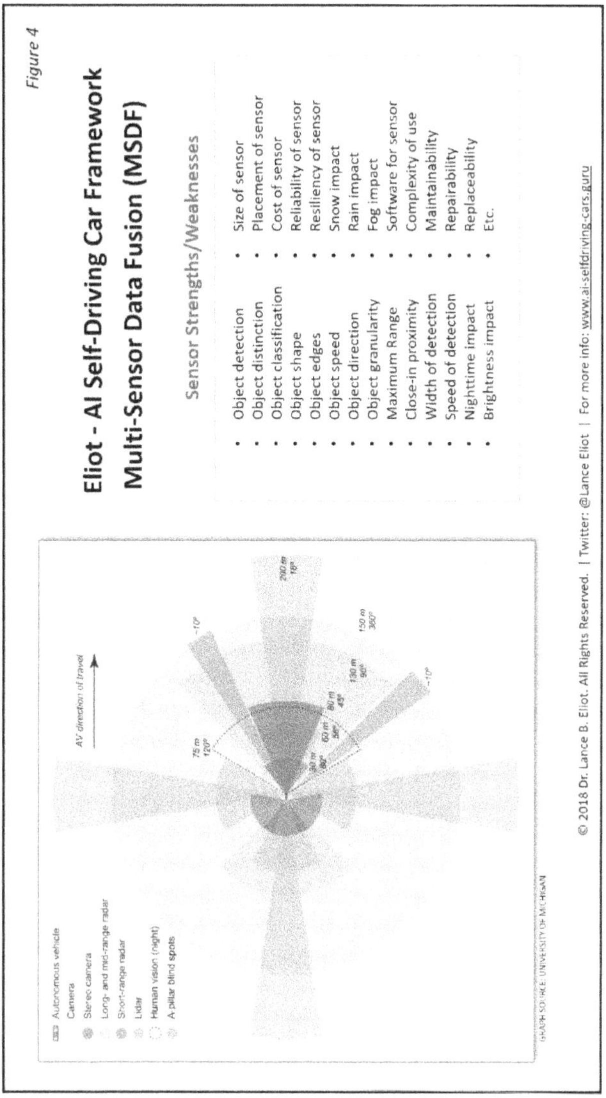
Figure 4
Eliot - AI Self-Driving Car Framework
Multi-Sensor Data Fusion (MSDF)
Sensor Strengths/Weaknesses
• Object detection
• Object distinction
• Object classification
• Object shape
• Object edges
• Object speed
• Object direction
• Object granularity
• Maximum Range
• Close-in proximity
• Width of detection
• Speed of detection
• Nighttime impact
• Brightness impact
• Size of sensor
• Placement of sensor
• Cost of sensor
• Reliability of sensor
• Resiliency of sensor
• Snow impact
• Rain impact
• Fog impact
• Software for sensor
• Complexity of use
• Maintainability
• Repairability
• Replaceability
• Etc.
Autonomous vehicle
Camera
Stereo camera
Long- and mid-range radar
Short-range radar
Lidar
Human vision (night)
A pillar blind spots
AV direction of travel
GRAPH SOURCE: UNIVERSITY OF MICHIGAN
© 2018 Dr. Lance B. Eliot. All Rights Reserved. | Twitter: @Lance Eliot | For more info: www.ai-selfdriving-cars.guru

Conclusion

It seems that the sensors on AI self-driving cars get most of the glory in terms of technological wizardry and attention. The need for savvy and robust Multi-Sensor Data Fusion does not get much airplay. As I hope you have now discovered, there is an entire and complex effort involved in doing sensor fusion.

Humans appear to easily do sensor fusion. When you dig into the details of how we do so, there is a tremendous amount of cognitive effort involved. For AI self-driving cars, we need to continue to press forward on ways to further enhance Multi-Sensor Data Fusion. The future of AI self-driving cars and the safety of those that use them are dependent upon MSDF. That's a fact.

APPENDIX

APPENDIX A
TEACHING WITH THIS MATERIAL

The material in this book can be readily used either as a supplemental to other content for a class, or it can also be used as a core set of textbook material for a specialized class. Classes where this material is most likely used include any classes at the college or university level that want to augment the class by offering thought provoking and educational essays about AI and self-driving cars.

In particular, here are some aspects for class use:

- Computer Science. Studying AI, autonomous vehicles, etc.
- Business. Exploring technology and it adoption for business.
- Sociology. Sociological views on the adoption and advancement of technology.

Specialized classes at the undergraduate and graduate level can also make use of this material.

For each chapter, consider whether you think the chapter provides material relevant to your course topic. There is plenty of opportunity to get the students thinking about the topic and force them to decide whether they agree or disagree with the points offered and positions taken. I would also encourage you to have the students do additional research beyond the chapter material presented (I provide next some suggested assignments they can do).

RESEARCH ASSIGNMENTS ON THESE TOPICS

Your students can find background material on these topics, doing so in various business and technical publications. I list below the top ranked AI related journals. For business publications, I would suggest the usual culprits such as the Harvard Business Review, Forbes, Fortune, WSJ, and the like.

Here are some suggestions of homework or projects that you could assign to students:

a) Assignment for foundational AI research topic: Research and prepare a paper and a presentation on a specific aspect of Deep AI, Machine Learning, ANN, etc. The paper should cite at least 3 reputable sources. Compare and contrast to what has been stated in this book.

b) Assignment for the Self-Driving Car topic: Research and prepare a paper and Self-Driving Cars. Cite at least 3 reputable sources and analyze the characterizations. Compare and contrast to what has been stated in this book.

c) Assignment for a Business topic: Research and prepare a paper and a presentation on businesses and advanced technology. What is hot, and what is not? Cite at least 3 reputable sources. Compare and contrast to the depictions in this book.

d) Assignment to do a Startup: Have the students prepare a paper about how they might startup a business in this realm. They must submit a sound Business Plan for the startup. They could also be asked to present their Business Plan and so should also have a presentation deck to coincide with it.

You can certainly adjust the aforementioned assignments to fit to your particular needs and the class structure. You'll notice that I ask for 3 reputable cited sources for the paper writing based assignments. I usually steer students toward "reputable" publications, since otherwise they will cite some oddball source that has no credentials other than that they happened to write something and post it onto the Internet. You can define "reputable" in whatever way you prefer, for example some faculty think Wikipedia is not reputable while others believe it is reputable and allow students to cite it.

The reason that I usually ask for at least 3 citations is that if the student only does one or two citations they usually settle on whatever they happened to find the fastest. By requiring three citations, it usually seems to force them to look around, explore, and end-up probably finding five or more, and then whittling it down to 3 that they will actually use.

I have not specified the length of their papers, and leave that to you to tell the students what you prefer. For each of those assignments, you could end-up with a short one to two pager, or you could do a dissertation length paper. Base the length on whatever best fits for your class, and the credit amount of the assignment within the context of the other grading metrics you'll be using for the class.

I mention in the assignments that they are to do a paper and prepare a presentation. I usually try to get students to present their work. This is a good practice for what they will do in the business world. Most of the time, they will be required to prepare an analysis and present it. If you don't have the class time or inclination to have the students present, then you can of course cut out the aspect of them putting together a presentation.

If you want to point students toward highly ranked journals in AI, here's a list of the top journals as reported by *various citation counts sources* (this list changes year to year):

- Communications of the ACM
- Artificial Intelligence
- Cognitive Science
- IEEE Transactions on Pattern Analysis and Machine Intelligence
- Foundations and Trends in Machine Learning
- Journal of Memory and Language
- Cognitive Psychology
- Neural Networks
- IEEE Transactions on Neural Networks and Learning Systems
- IEEE Intelligent Systems
- Knowledge-based Systems

GUIDE TO USING THE CHAPTERS

For each of the chapters, I provide next some various ways to use the chapter material. You can assign the tasks as individual homework assignments, or the tasks can be used with team projects for the class. You can easily layout a series of assignments, such as indicating that the students are to do item "a" below for say Chapter 1, then "b" for the next chapter of the book, and so on.

a) What is the main point of the chapter and describe in your own words the significance of the topic,

b) Identify at least two aspects in the chapter that you agree with, and support your concurrence by providing at least one other outside researched item as support; make sure to explain your basis for disagreeing with the aspects,

c) Identify at least two aspects in the chapter that you disagree with, and support your disagreement by providing at least one other outside researched item as support; make sure to explain your basis for disagreeing with the aspects,

d) Find an aspect that was not covered in the chapter, doing so by conducting outside research, and then explain how that aspect ties into the chapter and what significance it brings to the topic,

e) Interview a specialist in industry about the topic of the chapter, collect from them their thoughts and opinions, and readdress the chapter by citing your source and how they compared and contrasted to the material,

f) Interview a relevant academic professor or researcher in a college or university about the topic of the chapter, collect from them their thoughts and opinions, and readdress the chapter by citing your source and how they compared and contrasted to the material,

g) Try to update a chapter by finding out the latest on the topic, and ascertain whether the issue or topic has now been solved or whether it is still being addressed, explain what you come up with.

The above are all ways in which you can get the students of your class involved in considering the material of a given chapter. You could mix things up by having one of those above assignments per each week, covering the chapters over the course of the semester or quarter.

As a reminder, here are the chapters of the book and you can select whichever chapters you find most valued for your particular class:

Chapter Title

Companion Book By This Author

Advances in AI and Autonomous Vehicles: Cybernetic Self-Driving Cars

Practical Advances in Artificial Intelligence (AI) and Machine Learning

by

Dr. Lance B. Eliot, MBA, PhD

Chapter Title

This title is available via Amazon and other book sellers

Companion Book By This Author

Self-Driving Cars:
"The Mother of All AI Projects"

by Dr. Lance B. Eliot, MBA, PhD

Chapter Title

This title is available via Amazon and other book sellers

Companion Book By This Author

Innovation and Thought Leadership on Self-Driving Driverless Cars

by Dr. Lance B. Eliot, MBA, PhD

Chapter Title

This title is available via Amazon and other book sellers

Companion Book By This Author

New Advances in AI Autonomous Driverless Cars Self-Driving Cars

by Dr. Lance B. Eliot, MBA, PhD

Chapter Title

1 Eliot Framework for AI Self-Driving Cars
2 Self-Driving Cars Learning from Self-Driving Cars
3 Imitation as Deep Learning for Self-Driving Cars
4 Assessing Federal Regulations for Self-Driving Cars
5 Bandwagon Effect for Self-Driving Cars
6 AI Backdoor Security Holes for Self-Driving Cars
7 Debiasing of AI for Self-Driving Cars
8 Algorithmic Transparency for Self-Driving Cars
9 Motorcycle Disentanglement for Self-Driving Cars
10 Graceful Degradation Handling of Self-Driving Cars
11 AI for Home Garage Parking of Self-Driving Cars
12 Motivational AI Irrationality for Self-Driving Cars
13 Curiosity as Cognition for Self-Driving Cars
14 Automotive Recalls of Self-Driving Cars
15 Internationalizing AI for Self-Driving Cars
16 Sleeping as AI Mechanism for Self-Driving Cars
17 Car Insurance Scams and Self-Driving Cars
18 U-Turn Traversal AI for Self-Driving Cars
19 Software Neglect for Self-Driving Cars

This title is available via Amazon and other book sellers

Companion Book By This Author

Introduction to
Driverless Self-Driving Cars

by Dr. Lance B. Eliot, MBA, PhD

Chapter Title

This title is available via Amazon and other book sellers

Companion Book By This Author

Autonomous Vehicle Driverless Self-Driving Cars and Artificial Intelligence

by Dr. Lance B. Eliot, MBA, PhD

Chapter Title

This title is available via Amazon and other book sellers

Companion Book By This Author

Transformative Artificial Intelligence Driverless Self-Driving Cars

by Dr. Lance B. Eliot, MBA, PhD

Chapter Title

This title is available via Amazon and other book sellers

Companion Book By This Author

Disruptive Artificial Intelligence and Driverless Self-Driving Cars

by Dr. Lance B. Eliot, MBA, PhD

Chapter Title

This title is available via Amazon and other book sellers

Companion Book By This Author

State-of-the-Art
AI Driverless Self-Driving Cars

by Dr. Lance B. Eliot, MBA, PhD

Chapter Title

This title is available via Amazon and other book sellers

Companion Book By This Author

Top Trends in AI Self-Driving Cars

by Dr. Lance B. Eliot, MBA, PhD

Chapter Title

This title is available via Amazon and other book sellers

Companion Book By This Author

AI Innovations
and Self-Driving Cars

by Dr. Lance B. Eliot, MBA, PhD

Chapter Title

This title is available via Amazon and other book sellers

Companion Book By This Author

Crucial Advances for AI Self-Driving Cars

by Dr. Lance B. Eliot, MBA, PhD

Chapter Title

This title is available via Amazon and other book sellers

Companion Book By This Author

Sociotechnical Insights and AI Driverless Cars

by Dr. Lance B. Eliot, MBA, PhD

Chapter Title

This title is available via Amazon and other book sellers

Companion Book By This Author

Pioneering Advances for AI Driverless Cars

by Dr. Lance B. Eliot, MBA, PhD

Chapter Title

This title is available via Amazon and other book sellers

Companion Book By This Author

Leading Edge Trends for AI Driverless Cars

by Dr. Lance B. Eliot, MBA, PhD

Chapter Title

This title is available via Amazon and other book sellers

Companion Book By This Author

The Cutting Edge of AI Autonomous Cars

by Dr. Lance B. Eliot, MBA, PhD

Chapter Title

This title is available via Amazon and other book sellers

Companion Book By This Author

The Next Wave of AI Self-Driving Cars

by Dr. Lance B. Eliot, MBA, PhD

Chapter Title

This title is available via Amazon and other book sellers

Companion Book By This Author

Revolutionary Innovations of AI Self-Driving Cars

by Dr. Lance B. Eliot, MBA, PhD

Chapter Title

This title is available via Amazon and other book sellers

Companion Book By This Author

AI Self-Driving Cars
Breakthroughs

by Dr. Lance B. Eliot, MBA, PhD

Chapter Title

This title is available via Amazon and other book sellers

Companion Book By This Author

Trailblazing Trends for
AI Self-Driving Cars

by Dr. Lance B. Eliot, MBA, PhD

Chapter Title

This title is available via Amazon and other book sellers

Companion Book By This Author

AI Self-Driving Cars Inventiveness

by Dr. Lance B. Eliot, MBA, PhD

Chapter Title

This title is available via Amazon and other book sellers

Companion Book By This Author

Visionary Secrets of AI Driverless Cars

by Dr. Lance B. Eliot, MBA, PhD

Chapter Title

This title is available via Amazon and other book sellers

Companion Book By This Author

Spearheading AI Self-Driving Cars

by Dr. Lance B. Eliot, MBA, PhD

Chapter Title

This title is available via Amazon and other book sellers

Companion Book By This Author

Spurring
AI Self-Driving Cars

by Dr. Lance B. Eliot, MBA, PhD

Chapter Title

Companion Book By This Author

Avant-Garde
AI Driverless Cars

by Dr. Lance B. Eliot, MBA, PhD

Chapter Title

This title is available via Amazon and other book sellers

Companion Book By This Author

AI Self-Driving Cars
Evolvement

by Dr. Lance B. Eliot, MBA, PhD

Chapter Title

This title is available via Amazon and other book sellers

ABOUT THE AUTHOR

Dr. Lance B. Eliot, MBA, PhD is the CEO of Techbruim, Inc. and Executive Director of the Cybernetic AI Self-Driving Car Institute, and has over twenty years of industry experience including serving as a corporate officer in a billion dollar firm and was a partner in a major executive services firm. He is also a serial entrepreneur having founded, ran, and sold several high-tech related businesses. He previously hosted the popular radio show *Technotrends* that was also available on American Airlines flights via their in-flight audio program. Author or co-author of a dozen books and over 400 articles, he has made appearances on CNN, and has been a frequent speaker at industry conferences.

A former professor at the University of Southern California (USC), he founded and led an innovative research lab on Artificial Intelligence in Business. Known as the "AI Insider" his writings on AI advances and trends has been widely read and cited. He also previously served on the faculty of the University of California Los Angeles (UCLA), and was a visiting professor at other major universities. He was elected to the International Board of the Society for Information Management (SIM), a prestigious association of over 3,000 high-tech executives worldwide.

He has performed extensive community service, including serving as Senior Science Adviser to the Vice Chair of the Congressional Committee on Science & Technology. He has served on the Board of the OC Science & Engineering Fair (OCSEF), where he is also has been a Grand Sweepstakes judge, and likewise served as a judge for the Intel International SEF (ISEF). He served as the Vice Chair of the Association for Computing Machinery (ACM) Chapter, a prestigious association of computer scientists. Dr. Eliot has been a shark tank judge for the USC Mark Stevens Center for Innovation on start-up pitch competitions, and served as a mentor for several incubators and accelerators in Silicon Valley and Silicon Beach. He served on several Boards and Committees at USC, including having served on the Marshall Alumni Association (MAA) Board in Southern California.

Dr. Eliot holds a PhD from USC, MBA, and Bachelor's in Computer Science, and earned the CDP, CCP, CSP, CDE, and CISA certifications. Born and raised in Southern California, and having traveled and lived internationally, he enjoys scuba diving, surfing, and sailing.

ADDENDUM

AI Self-Driving Cars Evolvement

Practical Advances in Artificial Intelligence (AI) and Machine Learning

By

Dr. Lance B. Eliot, MBA, PhD

For supplemental materials of this book, visit:

www.ai-selfdriving-cars.guru

For special orders of this book, contact:

LBE Press Publishing

Email: LBE.Press.Publishing@gmail.com

www.ingramcontent.com/pod-product-compliance
Lightning Source LLC
Chambersburg PA
CBHW051047050326
40690CB00006B/635
* 9 7 8 1 7 3 2 9 7 6 0 8 5 *